SOCIETY, ECONOMY, RELIGION AND FESTIVALS OF TIWAS IN ASSAM

SOCIETY, ECONOMY, RELIGION AND FESTIVALS OF TIWAS IN ASSAM

Bandana Baruah

KALPAZ

Society, Economy, Religion and Festivals of Tiwas in Assam

ISBN: 978-81-7835-946-5

Published in 2013 in India by
Kalpaz Publications
C-30, Satyawati Nagar
Delhi-110052
E-mail : Kalpaz@hotmail.com
Leser Type Setting : Lucky Graphic, Delhi
Printed at : G. Print Process,Delhi

Contents

Preface

The objective in writing this book is to present to the reader the salient features of Tiwa society, its traditions, customary laws and culture. Each segment of India's population is as important in that it is a constituent part of a larger whole. For the enactment of laws, holistic development and progress of the nation an in-depth knowledge of the cultures of each of the social groups is of prime importance. The author has made an attempt to pen down her observations from that perspective.

The study has been divided into six chapters. Chapter-1 which is the introductory one deals with the origin of the tribe, legends and myths associated with the names of the tribe, Tiwa and Lalung, the source materials and methodology. Chapter 2 deals with the social life and traditional institutions, rituals pertaining to the different cycles of life-birth, marriage and death, status of women, dialect of the Tiwas and the differences in pronunciation between the plains Tiwas and hill Tiwas. Chapter 3 contains discussion on the economy of both the groups of Tiwas covering areas like agriculture, fishing, hunting, weaving and other crafts, livestock, trade and other economic activities. Chapter 4 deals with traditional religious beliefs and rites, acceptance of Neo-Vaishnavism by some plains Tiwas and their assimilation in Assamese society. Alongside, it deals with the spread of Christianity among the hill Tiwas. Chapter 5 deals with the traditional musical instruments and dances as well as the folktales associated with the observance of the various Tiwa festivals. Chapter 6 summarises the earlier chapters. The findings may help policy planners and administrators in taking appropriate decisions and measures for socio-economic development of Tiwa inhabited areas, some of which are in deplorable condition. A number of words from the the Tiwa dialect have been used. But no dia critical marks could be used. However to distinguish the pronunciation of (a) from (aa) single a is used for and double a is used for aa.

Acknowledgements

At the completion of this work I would like to convey my heartfelt gratitude and indebtedness to Dr. Swarnalata Baruah, Retd. Professor of History, Dibrugarh University for her constant guidance and professional contribution. To undertake the work I had to collect data from various libraries including Gauhati University, Department of Historical and Antiquarian Studies, Guwahati,Cotton College library,Tribal Research library, Assam State Archives library, Dispur, Social Research Institute, Kharguli, Guwahati, Morigaon District library, Margaon. I am grateful to the authorities of all the libraries for their help and co-operatiopn. I owe a deep sense of gratitude to all authors whose published works I had consulted and were a great boon to me.

I extend my gratitude to late Ganesh Senapati of Barupujia, Sri Mileswor Pator of Marigaon whose advice helped me tremendously. Rimol Amsi of Jagiroad and Maheswar Pator of Karbi-Anglong helped me with knowledge of Hill Tiwas. Ther were a host of others who helped me in every possible way. I ask forgiveness from all whose names I could not mention due to space constraints.

My experience during field trips interacting with Tiwa people in different Tiwa villages, with titular Tiwa Rajas (Chieftains) in their respective areas was a pleasant one. On the whole, understanding Tiwa society and culture has enriched me.

I express my deep sense of gratitude to ICHR for granting me financial assistance for this work.

I would like to thank my drivers, late Pradip Das of Hajo and Bhaiti of Marigaon who took me to different Tiwa inhabited villages.

I am very much obliged to my family who extended full help and co-operation to carry out this work. Last but not least I would like to thank the publishers for the trouble they took in publishing it.

Bandana Baruah

Abbreviations

ADGN	*Assam District Gazetteers*, Nowgong
DHAS	Department of Historical and Antiquarian Studies
HLG	*The Hill Lalungs*, Gohain
JB	*Jayantia Buranji*
JBAL	*Jagi Bhakatgaon Anchalor Lokasmriti*
KJK	*Kirata Jana Kriti*
LA	*The Lalungs*, Agnihotri
LST	*The Lalungs,* Sharma Thakur
MJL	*Morigaon Jilar Lokasmriti*
MSSP	*Morigaon Sahitya Sabha Patrika*
RRBS	*Rahar Rahial Barua*, Senapati
RRK	*Rahar Rahdoi*, Kalita
TSRG	*Tiwa Sanskritir Ruprekha*, Gogoi

1

Introduction

The North-eastern region of the Indian sub-continent is the abode of various tribal and non-tribal groups each having its own history, customs, beliefs, dialect, tradition and culture. Amongst the tribal groups are the Tiwas also known as Lalungs. The usage of the term Lalung is found in historical and governmental records, maps and monographs[1]. It is however a word of Karbi (origin) which was given to them after an incident which will be narrated later in the book. The members of this community prefer to be called Tiwa as it is a word of their dialect. However, while identifying themselves they generally say Tiwa Lalung or Lalung Tiwa. Both the terms are thus used simultaneously and indiscriminately and denote the same tribe. In this study however only one name, Tiwa will be used throughout.

The Tiwas are a branch of the Bodo group and belong ethnically to Mongoloid stock. They inhabit the plains and hill areas of Assam and Meghalaya and are called plains Tiwas and hill Tiwas according to their area of settlement. The majority of plains Tiwas are concentrated in Marigaon and Nagaon areas and are partially scattered in the districts of Kamrup, Dhemaji, Sonitpur and Jorhat. The hill Tiwas inhabit the hill district of Karbi Anglong and Ri-Bhoi district of Meghalaya. The Tiwas have been enlisted in the Scheduled tribe plains category but those living in the hill distict of Karbi-Anglong in Assam and Ri-bhoi district of Meghalaya do not fall into the category of Scheduled Tribe (Hills). In 1995 the Government of Assam constituted the Tiwa Autonomous Council in Marigaon district.

The Tiwa tribe as a separate identity is first mentioned in the census report of 1871-72 with a population of 34,859[2]. Earlier they may have been treated as Garos or Mikirs for their similar ethnic characteristics. Hamilton in his 'Account of Assam' mentions that most of the tributary Rajas on the south side of the Brahmaputra are of Garo origin and the art of warfare has hitherto made so little progress among the Assamese, that they have not been able to strip these chiefs of their dominions. On the contrary, they have concentrated themselves with a moderate tribute and conciliate the friendship of the independent mountaineers by a free commercial intercourse[3]. L. Devi writes "Side by side with the Mikirs dwell in the Mikir hills the Rengma Nagas (who are recent immigrants from the eastern side of the Dhansiri) in the Jamuna and the Doyang valley, the Dimasas or Kachari; in the Jayantia hills, the Kukis and the Syntengs; and in the Khasi hills and along the Nowgaon and Kamrup borders the Lalungs and a few settlements of Khasis[4]. According to the 2001 census report the Tiwa population is shown as 1,70,622 (Males- 85,964 and females- 84,658).

Origin

In all early writings the tribe has been referred to as Lalungs. According to Grierson, the Kachari (Boro and Dimasa), the Mech, the Koch, the Rabha, the Garo, the Chutiya, the Tippera, The Hojai, the Lalung and other allied tribes of North-East India belong to the Tibeto Burman branch of the Sino Tibetan speech family[5].

Regarding the original inhabitants of India, opinions differ among anthropologists. Whereas anthropologists like B.S. Guha consider the Negritoes to be the earliest settlers of India, others like Risley give their opinion in favour of the Dravidians[7]. S. Sarkar, D.N. Majumdar and others consider the Australoids as the autochthones of India[8]. S.K. Chatterjee writes that Negritoes were the first migrants to India and that they arrived in pre-historic times from Africa. The next people to come to India after the Negritoes would appear to be the proto Australoids and the speech family known as the Austric was associated with them and their descendants.Next in order were the Mediterranean's who in all likelihood spoke forms of a primitive Dravidian speech. The Nordics, the true Aryans were the last people to enter India through her western gates in pre-historic times[9].

S.K. Chatterjee opines that when the bases of the distinctive Hindu or Austric-Dravidian-Aryan culture were being laid that another racial (or, rather linguistic-cultural) group, the Mongoloid or Sino-Tibetan made its presence felt in the country. The history of the arrival into India of the various Mongoloid groups speaking dialects of the Sino-Tibetan speech family is not known, nor have all the various languages and dialects in the family been satisfactorily classified. It would appear that their presence in India was noted by the tenth century B.C. when the Veda books were compiled.[10]

Chatterjee opines that the part played by the Mongoloid peoples was confined to the distant eastern and northern frontiers of India – in Central and Eastern Nepal, in North Bihar, in North and East Bengal and in Assam. These he writes are rather far removed from the hub of Indian cilivilisaiton and history – in western India, in the Upper Ganges Valley, in the Deccan and in the Tamil land. The Mongoloid elements, again, because of their late arrival (they were possibly later than even the Aryans), could not penetrate far into the interior plains of India. Their earlier history was already obscure at that time, and still remains obscure.[11]

According to Chatterjee "with the single exception of the Khasis and the connected Jaintias (Syntengs) of Assam, the Mongoloid peoples who are found in India are all speakers of languages and dialects belonging to the Sino-Tibetan or Tibeto-Chinese speech family. The area of characterisation of the primitive Sino-Tibetan speech appears to have been North Western China between the head waters of the Hwang-Ho and the Yangtse-Kiang rivers. Mongoloid tribes from Western China speaking forms of Sino-Tibetan speech appear to have been pushing south and west from their original homeland from pre-historic times. The Tibeto Burman groups of the Sino-Tibetan speaking tribes would appear to have formed an area of dispersion in some tract to the west and north of Tibet (the present day Chinese province of Si-Kiang) from where they began to spread east and south[12]."

The Indo-Mongoloids have been referred to as *Kiratas* in the ancient scriptures. According to Chatterjee "It is the consensus of opinion among the Indologists that in Sanskrit the term *Kirata* indicated the wild non-Aryan tribes living in the mountains, particularly the Himalayas and in the North-Eastern areas of India, who were Mongoloid in origin[13]".

The name *Kirata* is for the first time found in the Yajurveda. The *Vajasenaya Samhita* and the *Atharva-Veda* describe the *Kiratas* as cave dwellers. The great epic *Mahabharata* mentions of several principalities all along the borderland of the Himalayas, ruled by *Kirata* kings. The *Kalika Purana* describes the *Kiratas* as having short stature, golden colour, shaven head, rough skin and addicted to meat and drink.

The Greek work *'Periplus of the Erythrean sea'* of the first century AD. knows of the Kirrhadai (i.e. the Kirata or Kirata people as a race of men with flattened noses, very savage living beyond Dosarane....... The Kirrahadai and their neighbours of the same stock participated in the little trade in silk that used to be carried on between China and India through Yunan, North Burma and Assam in the centuries round about the Christian era[14]. R.M. Nath writes ......' in ancient times, traders from different parts of Tibet, Central Asia and China flocked to Assam though various routes and as they traded mostly in silk, they were generally called Seres-Cirrahadoi (in modern sense Serek-cloth walla) Syrites-Cirata-Kirata[15]. Chang K'ien the Chinese general and explorer of Central Asia in the Second Century B.C. also testified that there was a trade between North-eastern India and South Western China through routes among the southern barbarian peoples which were not officially known to the Chinese ruling classes in the capital city in North China; this trade was in Chinese silk cloth and Chinese bamboo flutes among other things and it brought these articles into Eastern India, which were then carried through the entire length of North India to as far west as Afghanistan and Central Asia. The kinsmen of the Chinese, the Indian Mongoloid, or Indo-Mongoloids, were the intermediaries in this trade and not only did they carry material goods from China but also at times brought ideas, down to the second half of the first millennium AD[16]. It thus appears that the Tiwas may have come to this land by way of trade and finding the land suitable may have settled down.

Successive waves of immigrants entered Assam through various routes at different times. It is possible that most of the immigrants followed the courses of big rivers such as the Chindwin and the Irrawaddy, thus traversing through Myanmar (Burma) before entering India through the Patkai Range[17]. Another group followed the courses of the rivers Teesta, Dharla and Sankosh while still others entered Assam through the mountain passes. The Karbis, the Lalungs and the Boro, Kacharies entered India through the north-eastern route comprising the course of the Brahmaputra the Teesta, the Dharla, the Sankosh rivers[18]. All these people scattered themselves in various parts of the North-east and came to be known by various names like Boro, Naga, Karbi, Tiwa, Garo etc.

Legends and Myths

Almost all human societies including the Tiwas have indulged in traditional telling of the past to unify the people who ingrated at different lines through different routes, perpetuate continuity in the between the hoary past and the present and for a variety of other reasons. This traditional narration of the past is reflected in their legends, myths, tales, proverbs, riddles and songs.

Akir to other pre-literate societies of the world, the Tiwas too have acquired knowledge about their past, i.e. origin, migration, formation of village, circumstances of combat, festivals, customs beliefs through oral narratives and oral traditions. Oral tradition seems to have played a vital role is their everyday life as their source of knowledge and their constantly has not guided then in influenced them in their everyday lines. In their socio-cultural and political life, oral narration is still a powerful tool to prove or disprove contronersics and for resolving any mis-understanding.

The Tiwas have a plethore of legends. Legends land to make the past appear realistic and relevant. Legends contain some elements of truth. One legends states that, there were differences amongst the Tiwas over selection of *jela* (priest) when they were living in the Jayantia territory over acceptance of patrilineal or matrilineal system and they had two leaders Hura and Tangara. The former advocated patrilineal, while the latter advocated matrilineal system which culminated in a combat. In the combat, leader of particural group Tangara, was defeated and killed at the hands of Hura. His followers then left for the plains and while proceeding had to cross the Nilalung river with swift current in it. Many sunk in the waters while crossing the river but were rescued in time by the Karbis (Mikirs) who lived on the banks of the river. After that incident, the Karbis nicknamed them *langlung, lang* meaning to sink in and *lung* meaning man. From *lang lung*, the word may have got converted to Lalung[19]. Hura and his followers appealed to followers of Tangars not to leave but in vain. They were determined never to return and at a place called *Jong thang*, (South east of present day *Nongpoh*) they split a *kumura* (pumpkin) into two which indicated separation. Since water gourd was used for separatism many Tiwas do not eat this vegetable. There are some orthodox Tiwa octogenarians who do not go to the homes who grow this vegetable. This traditional story has been handed down orally from generation to generation which implies that the Tiwas were originally matrilineal and may have been influenced by the Jaintias in whose territory they first settled. However, since difference arose over acceptance of partilineal or matrilireal mode of irherilace section which prefered particrurial mode moved away to the plains. This oral tradition provides the background to the prevalence of matrilineal and patrilineal social structure even to-day in hill Tiwa and plains Tiwa society respectively.

This legend of migration when considered from the standpoint of separate plains Tiwa formation as distinct from those they had left behind may be interpreted as symbolizing their new identity, not necessarily associated with the etymology of the word Lalung. The migration aspect is woven around real historical events and have been preserved in the memory of the people through oral tradition. This is corroborated by historical evidence given in the *Deodhal Assam Buranji*[20]

Many tribal societies and the Tiwas too in their legends link up their past with Hinduism which was prevalent religion in the land to which they migrated. Seen from this perspective some legends may be considered as metaphors of the etymology of the word "Lalung". The mythical elements of the narrative reveal the religious consciousness which reinforces the collective identity of all those who adhere to it and thereby locate their ancestry in these legends of origin.

According to another legend, the Jiwas were ruled by the Demon King Bali who was a faithfull devotee of Lord Vishnu. The king wanted that all his subjects should adhere to the royal religion but a section of them refused to comply and their defiance irked the king.

As a punitive measure, they were compelled to wear a red imprint (*lal*) on their forehead and turned out of the land. Later on those bearers of red mark on their forehead came to be known as Lalung[21].

Again there is a legend amongst them that they were originally Kshatriyas and spoke Sanskrit. When Parasuram set out to destroy all the Kshatriyas to avenge the death of his father at the hands of a king named Sahasrabahu Arjuna, the members of this community went into hiding and escaped to the Lailung hill on the northern side of the Brahmaputra. They eventually stopped speaking Sanskrit and even forgot that language. When they returned to their homeland they were recognized not as Kshatriyas but were called Lalungs after the Lailung hill where they hid themselves[22].

Myths are sacred narratives sans elements of reality. In most of the myths, creation of mankind is attributed to the deeds of the divine and semi-divine beings. Myths in Tiwa society too lend credence to this. One popular myth prevalent among the Tiwas is their myth of divine origin in which they claim to be offsprings of Lord Mahadeo, their supreme Lord. According to this narrative, Lord Mahadeo created the flora, fauna and the gods. But the gods He created offered him no propitiation in gratitude. Offended He then thought of creation of human beings. He therefore set forth one day accompained by Bhagawati Maya and arrived at a lake after wandering around the universe. Being enchanted by the beauty of the lake he soon fell asleep on its banks. When he woke up he saw five drops of saliva which oozed out of his five mouths at the place where he was resting. (The Tiwas believe that Lord Mahadeo was five mouths). The Lord then created five male human beings out of the five drops of saliva. Seeing this, Bhagawati Mahamaya also created five females out of her body. The five males of Lord Mahadeo and five females of Bhagawati Maya then entered into wedlock. Their offsprings and descendants came to be known as Lalungs. Lord Mahadeo and Bhagawati Maya returned to their abode. The human beings had the unique privilege of seeing their supreme Lord Mahadeo with five mouths and since then propitiate Him with five sets of offerings. Members of this community believe that since they originated from the *lal* (saliva) of Lord Mahadeo they are called Lalungs[23].

A variant of this myth is that once upon a time Lord Mahadeo and his consort Parvati were enjoying the scenic beauty of Manasarovar lake. The beauty of the lake enchanted Parvati so much that there arose an innate sexual desire and hence sought the company of the Lord. But as the Lord was engaged in meditation He did not respond. Offended and enraged Parvati cursed Him to dewell in the South (*dakhin kool)*. When Lord Mahadeo woke up from meditation and learnt of the curse He accordingly proceeded to a high hill situated at *dakhin kool* (South). In the meantime Parvati felt lonely and depressed without her companion and became panicky. Being panic stricken she set fourth to *dakhin kool* with her compatriots assuming the name Jayanti Devi to find out the whereabouts of Lord Mahadeo. Lord Mahadeo then created a god Lungla Mahadeo out of his body. The union of Lungla Mahadeo and Jayanti Devi led to the birth of three daughters – Lai, Hillali and Lehi. From the eldest the Karbis originated while the Boro Kacharis and the Tiwas had their origins from the second and the youngest daughters respectively[24]. The woman here represents reproductive energy. The link of three daughters point to a common stock the Mongoloid.

Sri Sri Adijamal, an anonymous work published by Dattabaruah publication cites how the various castes and tribes of Assam originated from the various parts of God. In this treatise, it is also mentioned "*Laltit Honte Bhoila Lalung Utpati"*. Members of this community therefore believe that they originated out of the *lal* (saliva) of God[25]. This myth lends a quality of sacredness to augment the belief of their divine origin. In attempting to decipher the meaning, the question of validity does not arise.

Besides the stories of their early home, divine descent and migrations there are other narratives prevalent among them which serve as clues about their past. One account narrates that the members of this community were adept in the art of trapping elephants. They would trap the elephants by compelling them to fall into a deep ditch which they called 'lung' by using a long pole 'lang' in their dialect and hence the members were called 'Langlung' which in course of time became Lalung[26]. This account would make one believe that the Tiwas probably lived in areas also inhabited by pachyderms. They may have tamed them for their own use and probably hatched ways and means.

There are other stories regarding the etymology of the word Tiwa.

In Tiwa dialect. "Ti' means water and 'wa' means superior. Since they followed the course of water of the Brahmaputra and arrived at their present habitat, they may have introduced themselves as Tiwas[27]. Such stories indicate that they traversed a long way from their original homeland and that their early home could be somewhere north of their present habitat i.e. Tibet which was formerly included in China. G.C. Sharma Thakur opines that the word Tiwa may have been derived from the word Tibbatia meaning, people hailing from Tibet. In course of time 'Tibbatia' might have changed into Tiwa[28].

E.L. Dalton records a different tradition about the origin of the Tiwas. He states that the Tiwas are a breakaway branch of the Chutiyas and were original settlers of Upper Assam. Su or Ju means high or great. Su-Tiwa Chutia means the inhabitants of high hill or the great Tiwas. According to his version they lived at Sadiya once upon a time by setting up principalities[29]. The existence of a number of Tiwa villages in Sadiya could be a pointer in that direction but senior Tiwa gentlemen wholly refute this theory.

In a pamphlet written by Lankeswar Koch on the basis of oral tradition prevalent in Dhemaji area, the original abode of the Tiwas is shown as Tibet. The forefathers of the Tiwas are believed to have come in different groups and they entered Assam through the north eastern corner of India and settled in the plains of Sadiya and Dhemaji. These different groups were united by two powerful brothers who set up a new principality called Khola and ruled there. The older generation of the Tiwas say that the boundaries of this principality was Kapur dhuwa nadi and Obhuta Simolu on the east, Lothiya and Subansiri on the west, Abor hills on the north and Karhan river on the south. Obhuta Simolu is the present Bongalmari village. The Tiwa Raja of Khola principality had differences with the Adis, Abors and the Mishmis who resided that side. The Adis and the others used to indulge in loot and plunder in their principality and made life miserable for the Tiwas. Under such circumstances, some of them got together and moved away with their property and settled at a new place by setting up a new principality which included portions of Darrang and Nowgong districts and name of this new principality was Khari or Hillali. As days passed by, Hillali principality became very powerful and was a cause of envy to the nieghbouring principality. The neighbouring principalities therefore united and sent joint expeditions to the Hillali principality. The subjects of the principality then fled in different directions and took shelter in Nowgong, Mikir hills (Karbi – Anglong) and other places. There were some Tiwas who stayed back thinking that leaving their hearth and home would undermine their dignity. They therefore settled in the Hillalli principality accepting the superiority of the Adis and the Mishimis. Reminiscing their glorious principality, the Tiwas sing *La Li Hillali* which is their folksong. Some fled to Jaintia kingdom and the Jaintia King set up the principalities of Gobha, Khola, Nellie and Sahari for settling the fleeing Tiwa migrants. From such narratives it is evident that their migrations occurred in groups and at different times. The narrative gives us ideas of the direction and stages of their migration. Keeping aside their stories of divine origin it is justifiable to accept that they migrated from the land north of the present habitat which is Tibet. As the source of the River Brahmaputra is Manosarvar it is possible that they had to cross this river in course of their migration. Migration may have been in quest of food, clothing and better comfort[30].

In the land settlement Enquiry Report of 1851, it has been mentioned that some 'Lihing' kings granted lands to the Vaishnava Gossain and Mahantas. Historical records show the presence of chictairs Tiwa Rajas who how event but make no mention of Lihing Rajas. The word Lihing may be probably a distortion of the word Lalung. Again, another mistake seems to have crept in the same report which mentioned that some Salung kings ruled over the area on the eastern bank of the Kapili. But no tribe or caste by the name Salung has been found. There were however Lalung (Tiwa) chieftains who ruled over the area between Kolong and Kapili upto Dayang. As such it can be presumed that the words Lihing and Salung may have been due to printing mistakes in the record[31].

Objective and Scope

The objective of this work is to throw light on the migration of the Tiwas to the Brahmaputra Valley festival and to study their society, economy and religion which in a nutshell constitute their culture. The work aims at studying their racial origin, possible causes of migration to this land from their original homeland, their settlement patterns and place in the political history of Assam in the pre-colonial and colonial period till attainment of independence. The similarities and differences between the plains Tiwas and the hill Tiwas regarding their society, clan system, marriage, customary laws, economy, religion and cultural life have been approached objectively. The study also tries to probe how the plains Tiwa society was influenced by Hinduism resulting in Sanskritisation, and how Christianity left its impact on hill Tiwa society and how the traditional society went for a change through this type of acculturation. Attempts have also been made to study their political aspirations, the pattern of change due to modernity despite their efforts to retain their traditional system. The present work may help policy planners to get a correct insight into the history, life and culture of this particular tribe for adopting projects suitable to the local conditions and aptitude.

Methodology

The work is based on field investigation and published as well as unpublished materials. The dearth of written early history of the tribe was overcome through field investigation in course of which their folk literature and *vamsavalis* of the Tiwa Rajas were collected and studied. Interview with the present titular Tiwa Rajas (chieftains) enabled me to study some items of their ancient armoury and ancient ornaments which are still in their possession. Their rich folk literature comprising of myths, legends, ballads, folk songs, in brief, their oral history in which they are rich have been critically examined. I also collected information of the areas, which could not be visited through telephonic discussions. The *Buranji* literature of the Ahoms is the main source for getting an idea about them in the medieval period. Of these *Buranjis*, the *Deodhai Asam Buranji* which contains a chapter on *Dantiyalia Buranji* (History of Frontier Chiefs), *Jayantia Buranji, Kachari Buranji*, *Tungkhungia Buranji* and the *Satsari Aasam Buranji* were of great help to reconstruct the political history of the Tiwas in the medieval period. The records preserved in the government archives, including Tribal Research Institute, Social Research Centre, Kharghuli and also the libraries of the Universities of Dibrugarh and Gauhati were consulted. The Department of Historical Research and Antiquarian Studies, Asam Sahitya Sabha office, Guwahati, Srimanta Sankardev Kalakhetra libraries have all been searched thoroughly for materials. All relevant secondary works relating to Tiwa society and their folklores written by different scholars including the Tiwas have been consulted, mainly the souvenirs and journals.

Thus, all possible attempts to collect data from all sources have been made. There was no fixed framework or schedule of the field works but was undertaken whenever the opportunity arose and on getting information and invitation on the same. Care has been taken to collect relevant data for historical reconstruction and study on the tribe. Data thus collected have been verified by cross references and critical analysis. For the study of Tiwa society, economy, religion and cultural life, field investigation was substantiated with published material.

Source Materials

The sources of information for the study on the history of the Tiwas are extremely limited and scattered. They consist of both published and unpublished materials supplemented by inductive field work. These sources may be divided into two categories – Literary and Archaeological.

Literary Source

The literary sources may be further sub-divided into *Saci-patia puthis*, the *vamsavalis* of the Tiwa Rajas (all yet to be published) the Ahom chronicles, published materials preserved in the Assam State Archives, Dispur, published works of the District Gazetteers. The archaeological sources comprise of remains like the Sitajokhola, Mahadeosal, the sixteen stone sitting slabs at Silchang, the Jongal Balahu fort, the Basundhari *thaan*, the armoury of the Tiwa Rajas, the myriads of stone pillars raised by the Tiwa chiefs at Umswai market, Amri hillock, Suping Amkha etc.

Sacipatiya puthis has been derived from the word *Sanci* which is a variety of tree whose bark was earlier used for writing purposes. The bark was generally torn away from aged *saci* trees and dried in smoke by keeping them in raised platforms. After they dried up, they were mixed with alkali and the alkali was then squeezed out and were dried again. Next the barks were cut into the shape of parallelograms and straightened by putting weight over them[32]. On one side, preferably the longer side, in the upper portion some holes were made so that many such pages could be attached and tied together. One such page was called *pholak* resembling a page of the modern times[33]. When they were fit for writing and were written these were then called *Sancipatiya puthis*[34]. Some of these *Sanciputiya puthis* have been collected during field investigations. From these *Sancipatiya puthis* some facts have come to light. For example from *Sat bhuni* and *Baro Bhuni* one comes to know that Mahadeo, the Lord who occupies the highest echelon amongst the Tiwas created at first seven *kuls* or clan in commemoration of seven days of the week but later on increased the numbers to twelve in commemoration of twelve months of the year.

The instruments by which writing was done were *kaap* or pen made of bamboo or *khagari* (a variety of reed), *muhisunga* (a bamboo pot with cover for keeping ink, *aakmari* (bamboo scale) and *bindhona* (a pointed bamboo instrument for making holes on the papers)[35]

The traditional method of making ink or *mohi* was to dip a few fruits of *silikha* (*chebula* or *tormentosa, terminalia citrina*) in an earthen bowl for a few days. The bowl would then be exposed to dew for several nights with a non porous basin below it. The water would turn black and would percolate through the earthen bowl and drop into the non-porous vase in the form of deep black ink. There was another method of preparing ink and this was by taking the juice of *Kehraj* (*verbesina prostrate* or *eclipta alba*) and *silikha*, cow urine, bark of mango and *jaamun* (Eugernia Jambolana) trees all put together and boiled in an earthen pot. From the outer surface the vapour was collected and used as ink. (information collected from interview with elderly Tiwa gentlemen)[36]

The *vamsavalis* of the different Tiwa Rajas throw light on the genealogy of the Rajas who had authority over their men in different areas. I have managed to get the *vamsavali* of former Sukhnaguha principality of Sato Raja area. Inspite of my best attempts I could not collect the other *vamsavalis* as they were very reluctant to part with them.

The Ahom chronicles which include *Deodhai Asam Buranji, Tungkhungia Buranji, Satsari Assam Buranji, Kachari Buranji* and *Jayantia Buranji* provide much information on the circumstances which led to the establishment of Tiwa principalities in Ahom territory, the taxes they gave as tributary chiefs and the expeditions in which they assisted the Ahom monarch with their soldiers, the punishment meted out to them for betrayal during the later phase of the Moamaria rebellion. A.J. Moffatt Mills in his *Report on the Province of Assam,* 1854 provides information on the condition of the Tiwa principalities which were annexed to Nowgong district with the advent of British rule. The archival records kept preserved in the Assam State Archive Dispur, describes the role of Tiwas and the circumstances which culminated in the Phulaguri uprising of 1861. That this uprising was caused by the callousness of the Deputy Commissioner of Nowgaon district has been revealed from the confidential letters exchanged between persons concerned. The District Gazetteers throw light on the participation of Tiwas in the freedom movement and in Tiwa dominated areas.

Archaeological

In some places of Morigaon and Nowgong district archaeological remains of the period under study have been noticed. Temple ruins are seen at Baropujia- Mathorbori, Amlighat-Sitajokhola, Siva temple at Mahadeosal village – Jagiroad and a *thaan* at Basundhari, Jongal Balahu fort and an open air conference site at Silchang. Besides these there are many stone pillars raised by the Tiwa chiefs at Umswai market, Amri hillock, Suping Amkha.

Basundhari *Thaan*

Basundhari *Thaan* situated in Nowgong district in Sahari Mouza had been under a Tiwa Raja from the earliest times according to local tradition and oral history. On the bank of the Barpani river on a hill of huge boulders of granite stone are engraved two images of Ganesha on two rocks and another image of Jagadhatri on the third. The image of Jagadhatri is called Basundhari- protectress of the world. The Basundhari *Thaan* lends credence to the fact that the Tiwas wordshipped Hindu Gods as well.

Sitajokhola

At Amilghat on the bank of the Killing river about three km south of the National Highway is a hillock of solid granite rock rising gradually upwards from the river. At a turning point of the river, on its left bank, there seems to have existed a small temple on the top of the hillock, of which some remains have been traced. On the solid rock from the location of the ruined temple to the lowest water level in the river below, a flight of steps appears to have existed. The middle of the steps are overlapped with sand and vegetation. The Tiwas believe that Sita was exiled here and the flight of steps below was used to carry water and other essentials to her dwelling on the hill top[37]. This shows that the Tiwas have oral traditions among them associated with the epic Ramayan but this can be stated as a figment of their imagination as the episode of Sita is associated with Ayodhya. Such stories may have been told to the younger generation to inculcate the values of integrity with the country to which they migrated.

Jongalbalahu Fort

There is local tradition among the Tiwas regarding the antiquity of this fort situated in Nowgong district[38]. According to this account the fortified area known as Jongalgarh had been constructed by one of the Tiwas Rajas (Chieftain) of Sahari principality, Jongalbalahu by name, to protect himself from frequent Kachari attacks. This account states that Jongalbalahu was the illegal offspring of Gangawati the woman chieftain of Khola principality and Arimatta who was the chieftain of Mayong principality. Since they belonged to the same clan, marriage was taboo according to Tiwa custom but, as days passed Gangawati became pregnant with him and gave birth to a son whose name was Jongalbalahu. In due course the latter did not accept his father's property as a sequel to curses inflicted upon him by his father Arimatta and hence moved away and set up a new principality called Sahari. The same account further states that Jongalbalahu was a supernatural human being and there are many miraculous stories associated with him. It is said that he was so adept that he could run as fast as the wind, he could jump and sit on the back of wild elephants, he could swim across the River Brahmaputra and could accomplish many other incredible feats. Like his mother he was ardent devotee of Lord Siva and it is said that the Lord was so appeased with his devotion that he presented him a *toruwal* (sword) by which he could protect himself from all dangers. The Kachari Raja humiliated by his defeat at the hands of Jongalabalahu nurtured a vengeance and wanted to avenge his defeat and therefore targeted Jongalbalahu. The latter therefore constructed the fortified area to protect himself from such onslaughts. The Kachari Raja some say Meghnarayan while others say Gajraj even offered his daughter, Sukomola in marriage to Jongalbalahu to learn his prowess. He then succeeded in his designs and managed to procure the divine sword (*langkhui*) of Jangalbaluhu which was the source of his strength and ultimately defeated him. That Jongalbalahu was a Tiwa Raja is evident from their oral history. However at present there is a big state government fish farm in this fort.

Silchang Conference Site

At Silchang, on the side of National Highway can be seen an open air conference site where sixteen stone (*sil*) platforms (*chaang*) slightly raised above the ground exist even today. There is oral tradition among the Tiwa community that the Tiwa Raja of Khola along with his council members used to sit together to discuss important matters[39]. The Tiwas were settled in that area by the Jayantia King. At present the department of Archaeology has taken steps to preserve this area[40].

Mathorbori

There are local traditions among the Tiwas that Arimatta a Tiwa chieftain having committed patricide wanted to atone and absolve himself from sin[41]. According to this account he embarked upon several projects. In one such project he brought twelve priests and wanted to set up a *math* (temple) on a *bori* (mound) in the central portion of *pacho raja* dominated area in Baropujia but his attempted project somehow remained incomplete. A *thaan* (sacred place) instead arose in that area and that place came to be called Mathorbori meaning temple on a mound (*bori*).

Mahadeosal

On the side of the National Highway at Jagiroad exists a Mahadeosal. The place has a lot of stone round a fairly big mound. The temple is still held sacred by the Tiwas and many devotees other than the Tiwas too offer prayers and pigeons even to this day. The priest (*deori*) of this temple is still appointed by the titular Gobha Raja[42]. There is local tradition current among the Tiwas even to-day about the circumstances that led one Gobha Deo Raja Laising by name to construct this temple[43]. According to this account Laising Deoraja of Gobha had a dream in which he was instructed by God that he should set up a 'deosal' in the central part of his principality in honour of Fa-Mahadeo (the highest in Tiwa pantheon of Gods) and that a black humped bull, one white bearded goat and a pair of pigeons should also be set free. If he acted accordingly there would be bumper harvest and if not, drought and destruction would prevail.

NOTES AND REFERENCES

1. Sen, S, *Folklore in North East India,* New Delhi/Guwahati, 1985, p.113.
2. Beverley, H., *Census of Bengal*, 1872, Bengal Census Report, Calcutta, 1872.
3. Hamilton, F., *An Account of Assam*, London, 1820 reprint DHAS, Guwahati, 1963, p. 89.
4. Devi, L., *Ahom Tribal Relations*, Guwahati, 1968, p.145 (henceforth ATR).
5. Agnihotri, S.K., *The Lalungs*, Lucknow, 1996, p.161 (henceforth LA).
6. Grierson, G.A. *Linguistic Survey of India* Vol.III,. Part-II, New Delhi, 1967, p.14.
7. Das, B.M. *Outlines of Physical Anthropology*, Guwahati 1990, p. 94.
8. *Ibid.*, p. 232.
9. Chatterjee, S.K. *Kirata Jana Kriti*, Calcutta, 1974, pp. 7-11 (henceforth as KJK).
10. *Ibid.*, pp.14-16.
11. *Ibid.*, pp.18-19.
12. *Ibid.*, pp. 20-26.
13. *Ibid.*, p. 26.
14. *Ibid.*, p. 34.
15. Nath, R.M., *Background of Assamese Culture*, Guwahati, 1948, p. 15.

16. KJK, p. 35.
17. Grierson, G.A., *Linguistic Survey of India*, Vol. III Part-II, New Delhi, 1967, p. 14.
18. *Imperial Gazetteer of India*, Vol XIX, Calcutta, 1908, p. 224.
19. Barooah, D.P., *Assam District Gazetteers*, Nowgong District, Guwahati, 1978, p.118 (henceforth ADGN).
20. Sharma Thakur, G.C., *The Lalungs (Tiwas)*, Guwahati, 1985, p. 9 (henceforth LST).
21. ADGN, p. 119.
22. *Ibid.*, p. 9-10.
23. *Ibid.*, p. 10.
24. *Ibid.*, p. 9-10.
25. TL, p. 10.
26. Sen, Soumen, *Folklore in North East India*, Delhi, 1985, p.115.
27. *Ibid.*
28. *Ibid.*
29. Dalton, E.T. *Descriptive Ethnology of Bengal*, Kolkata, 1892 pp.77-78.
30. Deori M., *Tiwa Sokolor Chaamaadi*, Morigaon, 1997, pp.38-39.
31. Dharmaram Bordoloi, *Article in Ringsang*, 1973-74, p.156
32. Pator, M., *Pabitora*, Asam Sahitya Sabha, 1994, p.135.
33. *Ibid.*, p. 135.
34. *Ibid.*
35. *Ibid.*
36. *Ibid.*
37. Gohain Baruah, P., *Assam Buranji*, p. 15.
38. Kakati, Padmakanta, *Gobhar Lalung Buranji* Part-I, Jagiroad 1984 pp. 14-17.

39. Field Study.
40. *Ibid.*
41. Goswami, Decn Karunamoy Haripad, *Rupahir Purabritta*, Brahmananda Sewa Shram, Bhedowati, 1963, p. 37.
42. Field Study.
43. Gogoi, Lokeswar, *Tiwa Sanskritir Ruprekha*, Part-II, Raha 1986, p. 50 (henceforth TSRG).

2

Society

The primary objective is Tiwa society is to line co-operatively, harnorioudy and peacefully combined with humirty and dignity. Enery Tiwa individual is expected uphold Tisa societal norms and any deviance is dealt with. The word society has been variously defined. Ginsberg defines "a society as a collection of individuals united by certain relations or modes of behaviour which work them off from others, who do not enter into those relations or who differ from them in behaviour."[1] Giddings writes "Society is the union itself, the organisation, the sum of formal relations in which associating individuals are found together."[2] According to Mac Iver, "society is the web of social relationships."[3] Likeness, inter-dependence and co-operation are the essential elements which constitute society. In this context the Tiwa society may broadly be divided into two divisions-plains Tiwa and hill Tiwa, according to their area of settlement. Though some differences exist, yet there is also a strong underlying bond of unity between them. Amongst the plains Tiwas, there is, a further division between Saraniyaas and Asaraniyaas.[4] The Saraniyaas are those who have embraced Vaishnavism while the Asaraniyaas are the traditionalists. The Saraniyaa families have their own affiliation to different khels and no longer adhere to clans. The Asaraniyaas are organised into a number of clans or kuls.

Majority of the Tiwas are rural based. When a visitor enters either a plains Tiwa village or a hill Tiwa village, he would find several families living in a definite area having similarity in their way of living, speaking a common dialect, bearing either same or different titles, belonging to same or different clans, *vamsa* or *khutaas,* yet having a common village organization.[5] Generally the Tiwa villages are situated away from the main thoroughfares. The path leading to a village also passes through jungle and trees though these days much of it has been cleared. The path leading to a village is not blacktopped and gravelled but *kuchha*. In the habitation areas, loop paths branch out leading to the houses and to the fields. Villagers generally make an enclosure around their houses with split bamboos to mark their boundaries, to keep off pigs, cows, goats, etc. and also to protect their kitchen gardens.

Village Organisation (Plains Tiwa)

The headman of a Tiwa village is designated as *Gaonbura*. He is the representative of the entire village and is the liaison officer between his village and the government. However, the traditional system of social control in a plains Tiwa village is vested with the *doloi* (village chief), *buraakhel* (council of elders or village council) and *dekaakhel* (organisation of youth above fourteen years and not members of *buraakhel*). The *baarikhaa* is the village messenger. Generally in one plains Tiwa village, there is only one *khel*[6]. This *khel* is constituted by people belonging to three, four or more *kuls* or clans. It is further divided into two, namely-*buraakhel* and *dekaakhel*.[7] The *buraakhel* or the council of elders is the highest secular authority in the village vested with judicial powers and is comprised of eight persons. They are appointed for life and are selected from the *dekaakhel*. If a member dies or becomes incapable of performing his duties his place is filled up during the next *kheljaawaa* (the festival that celebrates the change in the dormitory system). Thc selection process is simple. The *doloi* who is the chief official of the *buraakhel* consults the members of the *buraakhel* and a day is fixed. The aspirants, generally former officials of the *dekaakhel* declare their candidature by presenting betel nuts and betel leaves to the *doloi*. If accepted, he will be taken into consideration. On the pre-fixed day, the *doloi*, the *buraakhel* and other villagers assemble in the *chaamaadi* including the aspirants. After discussions, new members are selected and the betel nut and wine offered by unsuccessful ones are returned. The meeting ends with a feast.

The *buraakhel* undertakes various welfare works of the village. Under the *buraakhel* there is another branch called *Ojha khel-phaao khel.*[8] The latter is formed by eight to ten elderly members. This *khel* trains the young generation in the art of traditional dances, songs, musical instruments, etc. In some areas, there exists the '*bhaandaari khel*', another branch of the *buraakhel.* In community pujas or functions arranged collectively *laopani,* (rice beer) betel nuts and betel leaves etc are arranged by this group.[9] The main function of the *buraakhel* or the council of elders is to settle disputes between villagers and to look after the general welfare of the village. The *buraakhel* takes cognisance of a wrong done in the village when a complaint is lodged through the *doloi,* who in turn takes the help of the *baarikhaa.* The matter is discussed before the council in the *chaamaadi* the next morning before the villagers set out for their respective works. The *doloi* makes a brief presentation of the case before the assembly and the complaint is directed to state his grievances. Before stating his case, the plaintiff shows respect to the *buraakhel* by placing a small coin on a banana leaf before the elders. The defendant is given the opportunity to present his version after paying respects in similar manner as his opponent. Thereafter the members of the village council discuss the issue and in case a witness is required, he is summoned by the *baarikhaa.* The decision is announced by the *doloi.*[10] He is responsible for implementing the decisions.

Dekaa-khel

The chief of the village called *doloi* carries out his executive functions with the help of the officials of the *dekaakhel* whenever necessary. The *dekaakhel* is a an organisation of all the young men above fourteen years of age in the village. This organisation exists both in the hills and in the plains. In the former it is manifested in the form of bachelors dormitory called *chaamaadi,* while in the latter the *chaamaadi* is almost a defunct body at present. The leader of the *dekaakhel* is called *chaangdoloi* and under him there are four assistants – *hurumaai, dangoria, tiluaa-khedaa* and *rebhaari.* Under the *daangoria* in public *pujas* the *hurumai* is in charge of rice beer, betel nuts and leaves. The *tiluaakheda* is in charge of youth dances, instruments, etc., and the *rebhaari* takes care of ceremonial dresses during festive occasions.[11]

The plains Tiwa villages have been influenced by the surrounding Assamese culture and no longer strictly adhere to the norms of their traditional village institutions. In villages with a mixed ethnic population, the organisational structure differs even though the Tiwas may be the predominant community. In such villages each community may have their own *khels*. The Tiwas in such villages use the large hall for meetings of the village elders, during festivals. The council of elders of various *khels* may sit together and discuss and decide disputes between the different communities that may arise.

Chaamadi or Youth Dormitory

In the plains Tiwas villages the physical structure of *chaamaadi* exists but the Tiwa boys do not follow the traditional norm of spending their working and sleeping hours there. They go to schools like other boys in the neighbourhood. The *chaamaadi* or the physical structure of the hall is used for discussing important maters by the *buraakhel* like *borkhel bichaar,* etc.

Borkhel Bichaar

The *Borkhel bichaar* is the traditional settlement of dispensing justice in Tiwa villages. As stated earlier, the aggrieved person submits a complaint narrating the details to *bichaar-maaji*, (chief judge) who informs the *chaangmaaji* and *garaimaaji* or the village headman.[12] The latter two then convene a meeting of the village elders – at the *chaamaadi* in the morning before the villagers set out for their respective work. The verdict is given by the *bichaarmaaji* and is binding on both the parties. Anybody violating or flouting the *borkhelbichaar* is excommunicated from the village. Such cases are rare but appeal against this verdict to another higher one does not exist. The cases taken up by the *borkhel bichaar* include theft, misbehaviour, violation of any social norm, etc.

The Raja (Chieftain) is responsible for administrating justice in the traditional system in the foothill areas of Gobha, Nellie, Khola and Sahari. The court is held in a specific place called *raajchaura* and is attended by the Raja and his officials attired in traditional dress. The Raja and his officials give a patient hearing and deliver judgement. The parties abide by the decision of the Raja but an appeal may be made to the village assembly after the judgement is given.

Vamsa or *Khutaa*

When one or more than one family belonging to the same clan have a common ancestor, their descendants are said to belong to the same lineage which they call *khutaa* or *bangsa* (vamsa).

Khel

When two or three *khutaas* unite on a common platform, that group is called a *khel*. Every *khel* imposes certain restrictions on its members. The members are to abide by its norms and if they violate, the concerned *khel* takes punitive action against them. The punishments include fines and the monetary fines go to the treasury of that *khel*. Every *khel* has its own officials.

Clan

Tiwa term for clan is *kul* and literally means belonging to the same blood. It is the most important social grouping amongst them. People belonging to the same clan consider themselves to be agnatic kins. In Tiwa villages, lineages bearing numerous clan names are found. An analysis of the stories connected with the origin of the. Tiwa clans suggests that a clan may have originated or come into being due to some particular historical happenings. Some indicate totemism, while sometimes a clan is named after an occupation. Some Tiwa clans have a tradition that they were named after the places where they lived originally. The origin of *kuls* is associated with legends. According to one such legend, to keep count of the seven days of the week, Lord Mahadeo at first created seven *kuls*.[13] Later on, to keep count of the twelve months of a year he created five more *kuls* and from these twelve there arose many branches and sub-branches leading to numerous *kuls*.[14]

According to another legend, in the beginning, there was only one main *kul* and from there branched out other *kuls*.[15] According to this legend, the chief of the Hukai clan had differences with the (*Baayu* Raja). In the contest which arose between them, the *Baayu* Raja tried to put down the *Hukai* chief, who always tried to assert himself. The *Hukai* chief would construct house but the *Baayu* Raja with his might would destroy it. Once, the *Hukai* chief got wooden logs from the hills and constructed a house and also got a wife for his youngest son. But soon after that misfortune befell upon him. The wind blew so fiercely that the roof of the house he constructed was blown away. Even people ran helter skelter. Some fell below the trees. Those who fell below the trees came to be called *Phangcho*. In this manner many *kuls* came into existence such as *Hukai* or *Sukai*, *Phangcho, Amsi, Amswong, Puma* or *Buma, Solo, Daam, Kashor, Dukhor, Mithi, Damang, Amfi, Masarang, Maserang, Muni, Daphorwali* etc. Members of the same *kul* or clan consider themselves as having brother-sister relationship. Since it is taboo for a brother and sister to enter into wedlock so is taboo to get married in the same *kul*. It is the *kul* or clan system which has kept intact the Tiwa society.

In the plains villages it is believed that clans descended from twelve sisters.[16] Each clan believes in its relationship with one of the twelve sisters, but when they migrated from the hills they were divided into two groups. Occasionally one may find a clan not claiming affiliation to any of these two groups.[17] Members belonging to *baara, na, saat, paach* adhere to figures twelve, nine, seven, five in all social religious ceremonies. These sisters were born on a red hill and as time passed, they came of marriageable age. Since they were unable to find suitable grooms, each of them thought of ending their lives by drowning. The water god, however, took pity on them and arranged their marriages with twelve young men. Twelve clans of the Tiwas thus arose from these legendary twelve sisters. Some clans originally belonged to other communities. For example, people of Kush clan were formally ethnologically different but integrated into the Tiwa society through historical contacts. In Tiwa dialect Koch is pronounced as Kush. M.M. Das and N K Shyamchoudhury write "It is quite likely that a contingent of the Koch army stationed there gradually identified themselves as Tiwas though they retained their separate identity."[18] The Tiwas believe that a man of *Kush* clan was asked to leave the village for marrying his cousin. The couple therefore left and lived in a forest. The wife one day gave birth to a male child while her husband was away to fetch water for her. Leaving her neonate behind, the woman went in search of her husband who did not return for quite sometime. In the meantime, a tigress looking for food happened to see the neonate crying and instantly began looking after him. The tigress took the baby and fed him with her breasts. In due course the boy left the forest and married in a Tiwa village. As he was brought up by a tigress, the boy was thought to be the progenitor of the *Mithi* clan. The Tiwa word for tigress is *misa*. It is quite likely that the name Mithi was derived from it.[19] In Baropujia, the people of Amchi clan claim to have descended from a monkey, but the tradition is that they got their name from a village in the hills where they lived earlier. According to another legend prevalent in the *Hukai* clan, one of their ancestresses Padmavati by name, gave birth to a tiger by her union with the moon. Formerly she was given protection by the Tiwas of Amswoi village since she was turned out from her own village. The tiger was allowed to go to the forest. Later on, Padmavati gave birth to a son from whom the *Hukai* clan originated. Since a tiger was born to Padmavati before the birth of a human, the *Hukai* clan members worship tiger. If they come to know about the death of any tiger, they observe all the customs relating to death ceremonies of old persons.[20]

The grouping of clans into clusters is essentially a local feature of the Tiwa society.[21] In each plains Tiwa village, the total number of groupings or clan clusters is collectively called *mahari* and unclustered clans do not normally exceed twelve in number. Members of a *mahari* are matrilineally consanguinous and all families trace their origin to a common descent from an original ancestress. In each *mahari* there is only one main clan and the other clans in the *mahari* descended from a female in the generation next to the ancestress. The number and grouping of *maharis* is not uniform. A *mahari* may consist of a single clan or of a number of clans. N.K. Shyamchoudhury and M.M. Das writes that groupings of clans into clusters could have been effected in two ways. The usual process has been the splitting of a clan as it grew in size and the other was forcible induction and integration of new groups into a numerically dominant and powerful clan. Such an example is integration of the *Kush* clan with the *Mithi* clan which are clustered together.[22]

According to another tradition prevalent in Baropujia village, the people of *Puma* clan brought under its domain the *Phangchongs* after a fight[23]. Again in certain clusters, clans are distinguished on occupational basis. Though there are thirty one individual clans in *maharis*, one clan in each *mahari* is predominant due to historical reasons. Names of these thirty one clans are given below, the dominant clan is mentioned first in each group[24].

	Clan	Sub-clan
1.	*Masarang,*	*Maacherang, Maagor*
2.	*Maadur,*	*Laadur, Puru, Chaangaaraa or Saagaar*
3.	*Maaploi,*	*Phaangchong or Fangsong, Pumba (Puma)*
4.	*Daafor,*	*Mithi, Lamphui*
5.	*Hukaai,*	*Khaaraai*
6.	*Amfli,*	*Aagaaraa, Chaancharaa*
7.	*Laasaa*	*Mithi*
8.	*Chaalaang,*	*Muni, Melaang*
9.	*Kaakhor,*	*Darpong*
10.	*Aamchong,*	*Aagaari*
11.	*Daarnong,*	*Daamlong, Kholar*
12.	*Lorom*	

Family

Family is the first unit of society. In Tiwa Society both joint and nuclear families exist. The plains Tiwa family is patriarchal and patrilineal. Formally there were joint families, but at present majority are nuclear families. A plains Tiwa family comprises of father, mother and their unmarried children. The father is the central and dominating person within the family and is also responsible for its maintenance. He has obligations in matters relating to the marriage of his children, performance of ceremonies and sacrifices and economic pursuits. His decisions in all matters relating to the inter-relations of the members of the family and management of the property is final and binding. He is the owner of all movable and immovable properties like land, livestock, foodstuff etc. Monogamy is the general rule but on rare occasions a man may take a second wife even though the first one is living. However, domestic strife or trouble due to quarrels between co-wives is unheard of. In the plains Tiwas villages from the age of ten onwards, a boy gets training from his father to play a responsible part in agricultural work. Girls of that age usually help their mothers in household chores. At present majority of the children attend school in their respective villages and also help their families in their spare time. So long as the children remain in their parent's house and do not establish their independent household after marriage, they continue to be economic asset to the family. In some families even at present the sons with their wives and children live with their parents and sometimes even with their grandparents. Such a family is called lineal joint family.

Within the Tiwa family, economic co-operation in the day to day life is maintained by every adult member. If the husband is busy in the fields, the wife does the household works like collecting firewood, cooking, weaving, etc. as in the past. She also helps in agricultural operations and goes for fishing, fish being an item of delicacy. She is laborious by nature and takes part in various economic activities like selling of firewood, fowls, *eri* cocoons, home-made rice beer. The income derived from such sales is utilised for running the household. The Tiwa women do the lion's share of the work but in the village council they do not have a voice. At present some educated Tiwa gentleman are employed in respectable Government jobs and live a well to do life.

Property Rights and Inheritance

In plains Tiwa village, descent is traced through the father. The property of the Tiwas include both movable and immovable items. The movable items include agricultural implements, musical instruments, utensils, dress and ornaments, livestock etc[25]. The immovable property refers to the land, both agricultural and homestead which belong to the family. After the death of the father or sometimes even before the land is divided equally amongst his sons. The father may keep one share for himself till his death for his own use. This portion generally goes to that son who lives with him and takes care of him till his death. The house too passes on to this son. Daughters are not generally given a share of immovable property but at the time of marriage, they are gifted with utensils and other items depending on the economic condition of that family.

Kinship

Kinship is a universal phenomenon that keeps human beings tied together in a common platform by various kinds of bonds. The most basic is the bond based on reproduction. This urge for reproduction results in two kinds of bonds namely, bond between spouses and their relations on either side, commonly called affinal kinship and the bond between parents and their children and that between sibling known as consanguineous kinship. The kinship system of a society lays down as to what should be the criterion of dealings with one's relatives both paternal and maternal. In traditional societies, social relations of the individuals are primarily regulated by kinship bond. G.C. Sharma Thakur writes "The kinship terminology prevalent among the Lalungs, particularly of the plains, may be termed as descriptive"[26]. Uttering of husband's name by the wife is taboo in Tiwa society. The husband also does not utter the name of his wife. They however address each other technonymically as *sui* and *si*[27].

Kinship Terminology

The Kinship terminology or the terms used in addressing relations are same for both plains and hill Tiwas. They have been mentioned in the latter part of this chapter.

Titles

The Tiwas use a number of titles in earlier days which formerly indicated social hierarchy[28]. The titles common among them are Deo Raja, Dekaa Raja, Paator, Senaapati, Konwar, Bordoloi, Doloi, Kaakati, Maantaa, Deori, Bharaali etc. The members of the Masarang clan take the titles Deo raja and Deka raja and those of the Kas clan take the titles Senapati, Das and Deori whereas those of the Amsi clan take Amsi and Pator titles. The Bordolois belong to the Laram and Paangsang clan. Konwar and Bordoloi titles are used by those belonging to Maaloi clan. The title Deori is also taken by members of Pumaalaakar and Munilaakor clans which are sub-clans of Maaloi and Salang respectively. The title Konwar is used by Melaang sub-clan and Lora is used by Daamulaakar and Damlong clans. Pator, Gaonkhowa, Dekadoloi titles are mostly found among Maadur clan.

Rites and Rituals

Birth

As in the past, the birth rites of a child in plains Tiwa society starts nine months before his or her birth. As soon as conception is confirmed, a ceremony called *nuanimanane puja* is performed for the deity Khamarina Raja who is believed to be responsible for shaping the limbs and other organs of the child[29]. The ritual sacrifice of a cock, a hen and two pigeons is performed in the ancestral house of the pregnant woman. As soon as the labour pain starts, all the members of the clan are informed so that they may take out enough rice from the granary for seven days consumption, since access to the granary is prohibited during that period which is traditionally called *Kecha chua*. The delivery usually takes place in the living room of the house. The pregnant woman is attended by two or three women at the time of delivery. They are called *ojani* in the hills and *giyaati* in the plains[30]. If the child is a boy, they strike a brass pot or a similar object to announce the happy news to the members of the family waiting outside. If the child is a girl, the attending women dance in joy and merriment. The placenta is detached with a sharp strip of bamboo. At the time of delivery a fire is lit in the room where the mother is kept and a piece of iron is put in it to protect the mother and child from evil spirits who is believed to be afraid of iron. As an additional precaution branches of certain thorny trees are placed on all openings of the room to prevent entrance of evil spirits. After child birth both mother and child are considered as impure and their movements and restricted to a room. Pollution or inpurity is cleaned or terminated after observing traditional costonary rules. The new born baby is not brought out in the open air for seven days, after which the house is cleaned and all the inmates take bath and wash their clothes. On the eighth day, a ceremony is performed to propitiate the deities for long life and happiness of the newly born child. If the child is a boy, the leading part of the ceremony is played by the *borjelaa* or the seniormost male member of the clan and by the *borhari* if the child is a girl[31]. Before the baby is brought out from the room a prayer is performed outside the room where the child was born. After the completion of prayers, the *borjelaa* takes the child to the mother and shows the assembled people. He then discharges four arrows from a small bow in four cardinal directions to make the child strong and brave. In case of a girl the *borhari* faces the four directions with the child in her lap and touches the shuttle and weaving loom or the handle of a sickle so that she could be an adept in her field of activities. This is followed by the *mitika maati diya* ceremony in which a small quantity of earth is applied to the whole body of the baby and the father or eldest male in the family recites a prayer[32]. To remove uncleanliness after the birth of a child, in plains Tiwa society, a social ceremony called *aaus gaara* or *ahaus kheduwaa* or *manshwaa* is held[33]. If anyone from a *khutaa* is to hold *ahaus kheduwaa* or *manshwaa* a person is selected from the *khel* convened at the *giyaati mel* and he is called *sajaati*. He is responsible for the smooth functioning of the *manshwaa* ceremony[34].

On the morning of *manshwaa,* the *barghar* is cleaned and wiped. The *jelaa* of the *barghar* sacrifices a fowl for the welfare of the *vamsa* members near the entrance of the *barghar*. Later on, the front area of the *barghar* is plastered with white mud by the *haari kunwari* and there the *jelaa* and *haataari* place *tulsi*, (basil leaves) and *dubari* grass on a front portion of a banana leaf. All those couples who had given birth to babies are required to give one bird each. In earlier times twelve hens had to be sacrificed if the baby was a boy and six if the baby was a girl[35]. All these birds are sacrificed by the *jelaa* with incantations. After the birds are sacrificed, the omens are read by examining the intestines. The flesh of the birds is then sent for cooking with arum leaves and chillies. When cooking is over, the *jelaas* of the *khels* are invited and seated in the front area of the *barghar*. When all the people of the *khel* come, the *borjelaa* would ask the *jelaa* of the *khutaa* the purpose of inviting the members of the *khel,* as a customary tradition. The *borjelaa* of the *khel* solves problems if there were any and soon after that there is invitation to take rice beer. After taking rice beer, on the directions of the *jelaa* of the *khutaa,* the hot chicken curry is partaken by all along with rice. All present pray for the long life of the neonates[36]. These days due to economic hardship, instead of chicken curry arum leaf curry is served and sometimes some families do not entertain with such feasts.

An important ceremony among the plains Tiwas is the *Khordeng-osa* or naming ceremony of the neonate which is performed when the child is between nine months to one year. Two or three *jelaas* take a child each and smear mustard oil over a baby by themselves chewing black pepper. Thereafter they call out names and by shaking them say *laanglou laanglou* which means be healthy, be fine. By whichever name the baby did not cry, that name is retained as the name of the neonate[37]. After the naming ceremony is over everyone present sings *La li Hillalli* their folk song in a chorus.

Another ceremony which is performed before the child is one year old is the *nabanaa* ceremony when cereal or solid food in the form of boiled rice is given to the child for the first time.[38]

Puberty

In Tiwa society when a girl attains puberty, only the mother and the elderly people in her house are kept informed and they maintain complete secrecy from others to avoid trouble. They do not perform any socio-religious functions for the same as is done in other societies. Generally, the mother manages the situation and the girl is kept very carefully. The village magician or 'bez' may try to take the water with which the girl takes bath after attaining puberty for evil purposes and hence it is important to be careful. In the modern times, the Tiwas, who have converted to Vaishnava *dharma* follow the custom of bathing the girl and performing socio-religious function called 'tulani biyaa' after attainment of puberty.

Marriage

Marriage is an institution which admits men and women to family life. This institution has social recognition and is a civil contract with religious sanction. The principal feature of the marital organisation of the Tiwas is the clan exogamy, that is, no person can marry in his or her own clan. M. Deori writes "Among the tribals (referring to Tiwas) if a couple belongs to the same clan, one living even at seven seas, thirteen rivers away on the other bank would not suffice for eligibility."[39] If one of them happens to belong to the sub clan, i.e., elder sister younger sister clan relationship (for e.g., *Phangcho, Aamsong, Puma*) the boy or girl's father and mother's clan would be taken with consideration and if it differs, then marriage may be permissible. However in such cases, the girl or boy after death does not get a place in the *haathaam* (specific area in the cremation ground for each member of the clan)[40]. Whenever any illegal union takes place, the villagers remorsefully refer to the *'Momai Bhagin Sila'* legend[41]. According to this legend, one Sola Sing married his niece violating the rule of exogamy. As a consequence, the villagers of Sahari compelled the couple to quit the village. Under such circumstances the couple offered prayers to the goddess Basundhari at Basundhari *Thaan* but their pleas were ignored and they were cursed to become stones for their sin.

Marriages in Tiwa society are solemnised after attainment of puberty. The marriageable age of boys normally ranges from twenty to twenty five and that of girls from sixteen to twenty-two[42]. Educated persons, though few, marry late. Child marriage is not prevalent. Monogamy is the usual custom but there some instances of polygamy. Widow remarriage is not encouraged. Intercaste marriages are accepted with penalty fee. If the boy gets married to a girl of lower caste, the boy has to pay a penalty fine, which is fixed by the villagers to avoid excommunication from their society. The practice of dowry prevails in some cases. The dowry includes land and items of household use, such as, furniture, radio etc. Cases of divorce between husband and wife is rare. However, in such rare cases, a couple may separate and live in the village without a formal divorce. Their status is equal to others.[43]

The study of the plains Tiwa marriages show that unlike Hindu society where marriages are solemnised before fire, in plains Tiwa society, marriages are solemnised before the *giyaati* of the concerned *khel*. There is a saying which goes, 'Raijei Raja.' '*giyaatiye Ganga*'[44] which means public are the witnesses while the *giyaati* is sacrosanct during that time.

M. Deori in his book '*Tiwa Samaj*' gives an idea of the marriage forms in Tiwa society. In plains Tiwa society there are mainly five kinds of marriages which are prevalent. They are (1) *Poluaai anaa*, (2) *Joron*, (3) *Borbiyaa*, (4) *Gobhia*, *Gharjiya* or *Ghorjuwai* and (5) *Dhori rakhaa*. Till recently the most widely practiced form is *poluaai anaa*; the next is *joron biyaa* while the third is *bor biyaa*. Though there is practice of *gobhia* or resident son-in-law system, it is extremely limited. Regarding two other forms *dhori rakhaa* and *dhoom biyaa*, these days they have become almost obsolete. In the past there was a practice of catching hold of a girl and getting her married but these days such a system has been given up. In *dhoom biyaa* the guardian of the girl fixes up her marriage without her knowledge generally with some one who has almost crossed his marriageable age. This is however practised very rarely.

The meaning of marriage in Tiwa society is '*Khule Mindaine dhaar saawaa*'[45] which implies that a girl is brought away from her *clan* and is made partner with a groom belonging to another clan. Generally only in *Borbiyaa* and *Joron biyaa* the hand of a bride is sought for. In other forms of marriage, this is not followed.

Poluaai anaa biyaa (Marriage by Elopement)

Romance between girls and boys generally begin at village fairs, theatrical performances, pujas and other festivals. If a boy is attracted by a girl he generally engages a mediator to know the opinion of the girl as far as marriage is concerned. If the answer is in the affirmative then there is exchange of *gamosa* (traditional Assamese towel) as a first step. Next on a pre-fixed day the boy along with his friends come and takes away the girl. The girl's friends also co-operate in keeping her safely and in a secret place for which they take a small sum as token remuneration and sign of respect. It is her intimate friends who help her in running away from home by quietly collecting her clothes and some money. As everyone in the groom's family is informed they prepare and keep ready the traditional rice beer. The day after the girl is brought or two days later, the *jelaa* of the clan as well as some elderly people of the village are invited to the groom's house for giving *dhar maghar* or good advice for leading a happy conjugal life, thereby accepting them as a new couple. At the beginning, the *jelaa* would enquire from the bride about the clan she belongs. If it is a different from that of the groom he goes ahead and further asks her if she came of her own will or if she was brought by force. In most cases the girl answers that she came on her own will. If both the girl and boy belong to the same clan, marriage would be possible only after certain formalities. The bride's mother or father's clan would be taken into consideration and if it is different then the bride would be placed in it, if, there are no objections of the people present. The assembled people would then give *dharmaghar* and give them social recognition.[46] They would be advised to lead a happy conjugal life. The next day, people from the groom's house would proceed to the bride's house. There at the house of the bride, people would gather and enquire if the customs have been followed. The fine for taking away the girl without knowledge of the family members is punishable with *haazaar tokaa*. The *haazaar tokaa* means a pitcher full of traditional beer with the mouth closed, a *saraai* (traditional plate with stand) full of betel nuts and leaves and five rupees. Later on depending on the economic conditions of the two families, days are fixed for *bhaar singaa* and *kush singaa*. On the day of the *bhaar singaa,* a feast is arranged for the villagers and the new son-in-law at the bride's house and after the *kush singaa* ceremony the marriage is held. The *jelaa* of the groom's side, the bride, the groom, the daughter, the daughter-in-law and others are present on the occasion at the house of the bride according to custom. The parents of the bride through the *jelaa* and in presence of people of both the bride and the groom would formally give away their daughter. The *jelaa* of the bride's side offers traditional beer to all present and sacrifices a pair of red birds (chicken) for the well being of the new couple. Some articles are given to the bride and the couple then comes back to the groom's house. At present most of the marriages are by this system.

Gobhia/resident son-in-law system

In the past there was the system of resident son-in-law in plains Tiwa families. Sometimes in some particular families the absence of a male child led to several problems, hence such families required resident son-in-law and if both the girl and boy agreed, such type of marriages were held. In this type of marriage both the boy and girl are informed that if either of them leave the relationship they would be fined *haazaar tokaa* and the couple is given necessary advice called *dhar maghar*. From then onwards the boy is treated or given recognition as a member of that particular family. At present such practice is rare except in the case of *haari kunwari*.

Dhori rokhaa or Marriage by Force

In this form of marriage, if a boy likes a girl, but the girl is unwilling, then she is forced to agree. In many cases there is no question of taking the girl's opinion, simply if the boy gives his consent the girl is forced to agree. If she cries and protests, the neighbours console her by saying whatever has happened, has happened. There is no use of crying. If the girl happens to belong to another village, then the guardians of the girl as well as the villagers go to the house of the groom and make an enquiry through a *mel* (gathering). In this *mel* the opinion of the girl is taken. If the girl states that she accepts her status and that she will not go, then the guardians of the boy makes arrangements for the formal relationship. The boy's family in such situations are fined *haazaar tokaa* as stated earlier. The groom offers beetel nuts and leaves in a big *saraai* along with a sum of rupees five, seven or nine and asks forgiveness in presence of the people of the girl's side. If the assembled public accepts his acts then the formal procedures like *kush singaa* and other customs follow.

Dhoom biyaa or Sudden Marriage

In this form of marriage, the opinion of the girl is not sought but her marriage is fixed up hurriedly (*dhoom*) by her guardians.[47] This is because the guardians have come to know about the illicit relationship of the girl or sometimes if the marriageable age of the girl has crossed. The whole arrangement is done quietly by the guardians of the girl and in this form of marriage all the customs are not followed. A few members of the *khel* and *vamsa* of the boy along with a few members of the *vamsa* and *khel* of the girl's side sit together for the formalities. Later on to get social recognition the marriage may be held. This form of marriage is rare now-a-days.

Joron Biya

This form of marriage is somewhat like the *borbiyaa,* from the beginning to the end but the *kush chingaa* and *bhaar* chi*ngaa* in this form are done for formality sake only. Though in the present, there is no custom of asking for the girl's hand, in the past such a custom existed. If there was any eligible girl, then the guardian of the boy, through a mediator would seek the opinion of the girl's family. If the answer was in the positive then about four to five persons proceeded to the girl's house along with a *bhaar* (shoulder load) of commodities which included betel nuts and leaves, *pitha* (rice cakes) and a pitcher full of traditional beer. On their arrival at the girl's house, the family members would make enquiries from where they had come, to ask for which girl etc. If the items were accepted, it is a positive sign. Very soon the other members of the clan were informed and invited. If however, the girl's family members were unwilling, then the commodities were not accepted. If accepted the traditional rice beer brought by the groom's party was served to the male members present. A few days later, the groom was required to spend a few days in the girl's .house to show his aptitude for work. But such a system is not prevalent these days. With the changing times many customs are not being followed. The *bor biyaa* form of marriage resembles the Hindu form of marriage and is practised by the well to do section. However, the marriage is not solemnised before fire.

Death Rites

Ceremones associated with death and funeral are experience, elaborate and sacred among the Tiwas. Death pollution lasts for several day and the Tiwas follow death pollution rules of the fear of the spirit of the dead and being haunted by them. A death in a Tiwa family is a burden some experience as it involvs the house holders with a great deal of expenditure. It entails on him to perform a number of ceremonies for at the propitiation of the deceased soul as well as to give a number of feasts to co-villagers who come to join in the mourning. Disposal of its deceased members in Tiwa society is done in accordance with certain customs. The Tiwas believe that at death, the soul gets detached from the body and hovers around the area where it used to reside while alive. The soul continues to live in that condition until ceremonies are performed and is sent finally to the land of the dead. The spirits of the corpse are very sensitive to any kind of neglect. The manner of disposal depends on whether the death is natural or unnatural. There is a belief that the soul of a person who has died an unnatural death never goes to the land of the dead. It remains in a miserable condition in the world isolated from its living relations. Such spirits are dangerous as they nurture vengeance against all the living relations. They generally stay in huge trees, in water and in out of the way places and when any human passes that way it attacks that person by diseases or death. Death due to old age or illness is considered natural and in such cases, the dead body is cremated. Both cremation and burial are prevalent. Formerly only dead bodies of wealthy and respectable persons were cremated but nowadays cremation is the general practice. The dead bodies of minors, accident cases, pregnant women, drowned persons and epidemic cases are buried. The suicide cases are also buried in a corner of the *haathaam* by purchasing a plot. This is called *Kaashlatit thowaa*[48] (keeping in a secluded corner).

When death occurs, the four corners of the bamboo mat where the dead body is kept are broken. The dead body is covered with a new white cloth. Then one person belonging to the deceased's *khutaa* circulates the news to other members of the same *Khuta* and also to every *jelaa* and *borjelaa* of other *kuls* of every *khutaa.* When the people receive the news they suspend all other activities and proceed to the deceased's house with a handful of rice grains which is their custom and assemble in the deceased's courtyard and sit in a circular manner. Then a *giyaati mel* to select a *giyaati* is convened to conduct the death rites. Formerly such *giyaati mels* were held in a central portion of a village or in a place where three roads meet. In the *giyaati mel,* the *jelaa* of the *khuta* is to answer certain questions which are asked according to traditional custom and the *jelaa* answers them accordingly. He can ask for help from others present for relief. Formerly the *giyaati mels* were covened in Tiwa dialect but these days in the plains, it is either in Assamese or both. Sometimes the *giyaati* is selected before hand and on the appropriate day, the *jelaa* of the deceased *khutaa* to get help from the *giyaati* and others offers betel nuts on a *botaa* (traditional plate with stand) in presence of the *khel* members. The person who is selected as *giyaati* of a particular *vamsa* or *khuta* is honoured with a *botaa* full of betel nuts and leaves by the *khel.* The *jelaa* of every *khuta* also directs one or two persons of their own *khuta* to carry bamboo and wood to the *maangkhor* (cremation ground). According to the directions, people proceed to the cremation ground. The Tiwas believe that *Fa Mahadeo devata* exercises authority over the *maangkhor.*

Generally there are two *giyaatis,* one male and one female. The female *giyaati* undertakes all the responsibilities in the house of the deceased till the body reaches the cremation ground. At the cremation ground, all the works relating to the dead is carried on and managed according to the directions of the male *giyaati.*

The *khel* advises both the male and female *giyaatis* to carry on their work sincerely. If any portion of the deceased's body is taken away by vultures, crows, dogs or foxes or any portion of the body is left behind by half burning then the *giyaatis* would be fined, which varies from hundred to thousand rupees. Such money has to be placed on a *botaa* over the betel nuts and leaves and has to be offered in presence of the *khel* members in a submissive manner. If one belongs to *saat bhuni* then seven leaves and seven betel nuts, if nine, then nine betel leaves and nuts and if twelve then twelve betel leaves and nuts together with *edhaar mod* (sufficient quantity of rice beer) for all members of the *khel* or *vamsa*). Depending on the *khel* concerned, the amount of monetary fine varies. The offering of money on betel nuts and leaves in a *botaa* is called *haatir pitheet mout diya* in plains Tiwa villages.

The *giyaati* proceeds to the cremation ground (*maangkhor*) with *harputi* (thatched torch) in hand and sets up a pyre in the *haathaam*. *Maangkhor* which is also called *maangkor* or *maakor* by some Tiwas is set up by the *borjelaa, loro* and *jelaas* of every *khutaa* belonging to different clans. It is generally situated near streams or a pond is dug nearby. Water from the pond is used to put out the fire on the pyre when everything is over. Every clan has its own specified area in the cremation ground where they cremate the dead and each of these specified places is called *haathaam*. There is a procedure followed to select *haathaam*. It is selected by the *jelaa* of the *barghar* and in some places on the direction of the *jelaa* of the *barghar*, the *giyaati* of the clan or any member of a *khel* may also choose. He places on a bunch of banana leaves, some basil (*tulsi)* leaves, *dubari* grass and betel nuts and leaves and by offering prayers to their respective *kul devatas* and their ancestors throws a hen's egg wrapped in seven or nine rounds of thread within the *maangkhor*. This process is called *Tudi Kaawaa, tudi* means egg and *kaawaa* means to throw.[49] At whichever place the egg falls that particular place is selected as *haathaam* for that particular clan. The *haathaam* has great sentimental value for the Tiwas because it is here that all the bones of the same clan get together and thus unites the dead with the ancestors. Under the *haathaam*, stones and snails are placed. It is an offence to cremate a person belonging to another clan in the *haathaam* of a particular clan. If a married girl's *kulsingaa* ceremony was not performed then she may be cremated in the *haathaam* of her parents. But married woman whose *kulsingaa* ceremony is performed cannot be cremated in her parent's *haathaam*. They are to be cremated in the *haathaam* of their husband only. Women who have *gobhia* or resident husbands do not undergo *kulsinga* ceremony. Formerly, *kulsinga* ceremony was performed soon after marriage. This was to facilitate the first born child of the new couple to be adopted by the maternal uncle (mother's brother) when the child grew up. The adopted nephew would get the *kul* and *haathaam* of his uncle. The nephew would also get the inheritance rights of the uncle's property. This system is called *Jara Saja* or *Jara Tana* but is no longer in vogue at present.

The funeral pyre is generally set up facing the north eastern direction. This is not only in case of human beings but in case of domestic animals too. For the members belonging to *Maaloi, Masarang, Maserang* and *Muni,* nine layers of wood are necessary. Rest of the *kuls* (clans) use seven layers of wood. While making the *chaangi* (improvised bamboo bed for carrying the dead body from the house to the cremation ground) also, tradition has to be strictly maintained.

As soon as the work of the pyre is over the *giyaati* informs the villagers to bring the dead body to the *maangkhor*. The dead body is kept inside the house till it is taken to the cremation ground and even if family members know that a person will die he or she as the case may be, is not taken outside the house. The Tiwas believe that just as a person lived in that house he or she also has a right to die in that house.[50] Formerly all dead bodies were washed over a wooden piece with a mixture of fine ground, gram and raw grated turmeric. Oil was then applied after placing the body on a *dhaari* (mat) and new clothes were placed by family members. These days the dead bodies of only respectable persons are washed. This is done by the female *giyaati.* In case of death of married women, a big vermillion tika was applied to the forehead. But this is not done in case of widows.

In the meantime, the female *giyaati* prepares a boiled meal for the dead which constitutes rice, egg and white brinjal in a mud container. The hill Tiwas do not use brinjal. The cooked items are then placed on a *khoraahi* (bamboo made object) which is covered with plantain leaves and taken from the home and placed in a corner of the garden. After that it is offered to the dead in a north-eastern direction. The deceased is offered rice, egg, rice beer and water. These items are also taken to the *maangkhor* and placed on the ground below where the head is placed. The family members and close relatives may then offer food to the dead with the left hand one by one.

While taking out the dead body or carrying it to the cremation ground, the legs should be on the front and the head on the rear. The body should be tied to the *chaangi*. When the *chaangi* is taken on the shoulders, an egg is broken below the *chaangi* symbolizing the end of life. In the plains before taking the dead body on the shoulders seven or nine times backward and forward movement of the *chaangi* is made. This is called *Lusiwa*.[51] In the foothill areas and hill villages this is done near the door while taking out the dead body from inside. They call it *nunsiyoy*.[52] While the backward and forward movement is in progress, one of the on-lookers utters.... *Manuhe maarileo marile, dewe maarileo marile, Lora aase, maati aase, kheti aase, baati aase, Ajir poraa aaru hes nakaribi, thel, nakaribi, duar khurkhuriai nethaakibi, laugaraa khukuriai nethaakibi, Ajir poraa aaru ghar baari erili, Faamaari hoi aahi aamoni kari aasuti kari nethakibi,* meaning whoever might be responsible for your death, you are no more with us. You have left your sons, grandsons, bullocks and cows, agricultural lands and everything you possessed during your life time. Do not disturb them by appearing as evil spirits. After this all the villagers who are present in the courtyard, pay their last regards to the dead by bowing their heads.

The female *giyaati* takes some white threads and while going ahead of the dead body wraps the threads on the grass. It is believed that by walking over the threads, the soul of the dead will be able to cross the dangerous rivers on the way to the other world. In some villages, the female *giyaati* spreads some puffed fried rice grains (*aakhoi*) on the way to the cremation ground in the belief that the dead will get all pomp and pleasures in the next life if it walks over them.

Before placing the dead body over the pyre, the body is moved forward and backward (*lusiyay*) for seven or nine times depending on the affiliation to the *bhuni*. In some areas, the dead body is taken around the pyre for seven or nine times. The *giyaati* first applies fire over the face of the dead body. The faces of males should be kept upwards while those of females downwards. After the *giyaati* others may apply fire in the face of the dead body. When the burning of the body is complete, a human shape is made out of the ashes. Two small reeds are placed in the two nasal holes. The cooked food and rice brought to the cremation ground are placed over the symbol. The *giyaati* then utters the following: *Maanuse maarileo nejanu, Dewe maarileo nejanu, Manuse maarise jodi sihaator kaandhe uthibi, Aamoni karibi, Asuti karibi, jodi Dewe Marise, Tenehole Dewatar goi tu tibaa, faan Tutibaa, Yaar para Aamaar Aaru koba loga nai, Aajir para aamaar lagat sambandha sesh hoise, Faamaari hoi gharar̀ lerela sepeta naaduni, aanak bhoy nukhuwaabi, nijor dharma nije raakhibi,* meaning we do not know whether you have been killed by a man or a deity. If you are killed by men then disturb them always, if however a deity has killed you, then the deity will be deprived of his *puja*. We do not want to say anything more. From today you have cut all connections with us. Do not disturb the little children by taking shape of an evil spirit. Maintain your own principles.[54]

When respectable Tiwa personalities expire, apart from the person who generally circulates the news, the *bordhulia* of the *khel* beats the *khraambaar* (drum) in a particular manner and conveys the death to everyone[55]. When people hear the *khraambaar* beaten in this manner, they become alert that some notable person has passed away. The dead body of such respectable persons is smeared with sandal paste and along with incense sticks and *dhunaa* (*canaries resimiferum*) flowers are placed on the body. On all four sides of the *chaangi,* flower garlands are hung. When the body is taken to the cremation ground, in front, the drum beaters beat the *khraambaar,* (big drum) *khraam,* (small drum) *pisukhraam* (kettle drum), the *kaali (pipe)* and proceed in a procession. All the instrumentalists are to continue till fire is applied to the mouth of the dead body. These instruments are purified by sprinkling water mixed with copper and basil leaves and are then again kept in their assigned place.

When a Raja (chieftain) dies, his body cannot be taken to the cremation ground before his successor is appointed. The new Raja offers betel nuts and leaves near the dead body of the Raja by prostrating before him and asking for the *Raajpad* or the Chieftain's post. Before the body is placed on the pyre, his head is placed in a north-eastern direction and backward and forward movements are done as stated above adhering strictly to the number of times to which his clan is affiliated. The *giyaati* first applies fire to the mouth of the deceased in the pyre. Later on the relatives may do it.

While the body of the dead keeps burning it is considered ill for the family if bamboo bursts and makes sound.[56] The joints of the bamboos are therefore cut before being placed on the fire. If the eyes burst and makes noise, it is considered as a bad sign for other family members. In anger sometimes one Tiwa man may curse another by saying that when he dies may his eyes burst. Sometimes faces of dead persons do not burn easily and the Tiwas believe that it is because of their misdeeds. They also believe that faces of people knowing *baaro bhuyaan geet* or *baaro kulia geet* do not burn easily.

The people believe in the existence of evil spirits and therefore take precaution particularly when they return from cremation ground. Halfway after returning they light a *harputi* and place dried leaves, branches of trees etc., and jump over that fire and do not look backwards any more. Purification of the members returning from the cremation ground is done by a particular *kul* (clan) in plains Tiwa village. For rendering such service they are to receive *edhaar mod* (sufficient quantity of rice beer for consumption of all members of their *khel*) customarily in a year.

A few elderly persons of that *khel* prepare a mixture of water, *tulsi* leaf, *dubari* grass and cowdung in a pot and sprinkle the mixture over the persons. A fire is arranged in the entrance of the village and the participants jump over it. The Tiwas believe that evil spirits cannot come by jumping over fire. The entrance of their respective houses are also sprinkled with *tulsi, dubari* and cow dung mixed water. They take bath before entering their respective houses.

Again all members assemble in the courtyard of the deceased on the invitation of the *borjelaa* of the *khel*. The *jelaas* of other *khutas* also come and sit in a circular way. The *giyaati* is asked if everything was done at the directions of the *borjelaa*. In the meantime, the whole house is cleaned and floors wiped including cowshed and the clothes are washed. The *giyaati* is to sit in a north eastern direction. The *borjelaa* of the *khel* and other *jelaas* must sit in an eastern direction of the deceased *khuta's jelaa*. The female *giyaati* sits inside. The heir of the deceased keeps one pot of *pohon mod* (rice beer which is strong,) some salt, a bunch of betel nuts, five packets of betel, some clothes and ornaments and other articles in a banana leaf. After some discussions *pohon mod* is served and the articles are distributed. Special clothes like *cheleng kapoor* and *mekhela* are presented to the male and female *giyaaties* respectively. Sometimes presents like utensils, cattle etc, are also presented. At the directions of the *borjelaa,* the young boys and girls perform *naam kirton* for three to four days. On the eighth day after taking fish prepared with alkali *(khaar maas)* normal food is resumed by the bereaved members. In the intervening period, only fruits and light meals are taken without oil and turmeric powder. The main death ceremony or *karam* may be solemnized individually or jointly by a *vamsa* which may be done immediately or kept pending for about a year as it is an expensive affair.

Karam

Karam ceremony as stated earlier, in the plains Tiwa villages may be performed individually or jointly. It is sometimes held jointly because the *karam* which is to be performed after death was kept pending. As it was kept suspended the custom is called *tuli thowa prothaa.*[57] On this occasion food and drinks (rice beer) called *pinda* are offered to the departed soul or souls. When the decision is taken to hold the ceremony jointly all the members of the clan including those of other clans are informed at least ten or fifteen days in advance. All the families in which death had occurred in the recent years contribute to the common fund of the *karam*. Earlier *karam* was a seven day function but these days it is a one to two days affair. Formerly five pigs were essential for this ceremony but at present due to economic hardship *karam* is observed with one pig and five fowls only. Every *vamsa* member has to bring one *bhaar* which contains one basketful of rice, one pot of *zu*, a bunch of nuts and five bundles of betel leaves.

The *giyaati,* both male and female play important roles in the *karam*. The *giyaatis* are appointed by the *khel* on the request of the *vamsa,* who take charge at least three days ahead of the ceremony.

During these days the female *giyaati* cooks meals for all the members.

On the day of *karam*, the male *giyaati* shaves the hair of the sons of the deceased. Nowadays the *giyaati* nominally cuts the hair and after that the hair dressers complete it. After this is over, the *giyaatis* take ceremonial bath. Killing of pigs on this occasion is an unavoidable part of the *karam* ceremony. For this occasion the *gharburaa* of the *vamsa* takes out the *zelaa* or arrow from the altar of the *barghar* for piercing the pig and place it in the courtyard already purified with sacred water. The pig is bathed and placed over a bundle of banana leaves. Some rice and *dubari* grass are put on its back. The family or families on whose behalf the *karam* is held, bow down before the elders and the pig. The *gharburaa* takes the *zeal* (sacred arrow) in his hand and bows to six directions before piercing the pig. If the first attempt is a failure he has to take permission from the elderly persons for a second attempt by showing due respect to them. Whether he succeeds in first or second attempt the arrow must not be removed till the pig dies. As soon as they are convinced that the pig is dead the *gharburaa* pulls out the arrow and after washing it puts it back in the *barghar*. Some persons in a jovial manner may obstruct the *gharburaa* who then explains the reason of removal of the *zela*. The pig is cut into pieces and one portion is taken inside the *barghar* where the female *giyaati* cooks it for the dead persons. The *giyaati* also prepares rice and alkaline curry to be offered to the dead. The *randhani* (cook) and the *deori* prepare a general feast in the courtyard where pork forms a special item.

The female *giyaati* collects the cooked food and other items in a banana leaf near the *thunaakhutaa* and offers this *pinda* pronouncing the names of the dead persons or person on whose behalf the *karam* is held. After that, the sons and other relatives of the deceased offer *pinda*. When all the relatives complete their offering of *pinda*, the *giyaati* takes the *pinda* to the *maakor* or cremation ground and keeps it for the deceased under a tree. Then all the assembled villagers take part in the feast. The *giyaatis* are duly honoured for their services. Both cash and kind are given to them in lieu of the services rendered. The occasion comes to an end with the *sumsira pansira* ceremony, when each of the elderly members is given a piece of betel nut and one betel leaf on a banana leaf. The nut is thrown away and the betel leaf is torn into pieces. The Tiwas believe that if they do this dead persons do not disturb the members of the family. On the same or the following day one hind leg of the pig and one pot of *zu* are sent to the house of the male *giyaati* who shares these with the co-villagers.

Traditional Beliefs Regarding the Dead

The Tiwas cling to certain beliefs handed down to them generation after generation orally. They believe that death is delayed because of illegal or unjust activities during a persons life time. It is also believed that one suffers at the time of death because of his participation in crime although he might not have committed the crime himself. If a person expires with unfulfilled desires his soul soon gets rebirth. If however rebirth does not take place soon, then his soul would disturb the people in the form of evil spirits (*faamaari*). Bursting of eyes while being consigned to flames indicates that the soul will not be free from rebirth. The faces of people who are not pure in heart do not burn easily. If a face does not get burnt easily it is also believed that the deceased may have had a desire to see someone and so a timber is placed on the pyre.[58]

Death on Tuesday or Saturday is not considered auspicious for the family. After seven days of the death, the elderly members of the family go to the cremation ground and observe the cooked food served to the dead kept close to the place of cremation. If it remains untouched, it is believed that some close relatives may die or the village would be affected by natural calamities. Death may be caused because of envy, revenge etc, by other persons who may apply poison without knowledge of the deceased by offering him betel leaves and betel nuts mixed with *lakam*, which is a poisonous herb. The victim takes it innocently without suspicion and dies after some months. The *ojha* (magician) is consulted to ascertain the cause of death.

Concept of Soul

The Tiwas believe that the soul embodies the heart and at the time of death it goes out through the eyes.[59] The soul continues to exist even after death. They believe in a land of the dead which can be reached by a difficult path often guarded by some spirits of the other world who examine the soul's identity before admitting it. They also believe in the immortality of the soul.

Concept of Spirit

There are places like the cremation ground which are not frequented by people, such places are believed to be the abode of the evil spirits. If a person falls ill after visiting such places, it is believed that he was attacked by evil spirits which is the cause of his death.[60]

Folk Beliefs

Every community has its age old beliefs and practices which are handed down orally from one generation to the next and the Tiwas are no exception. The Tiwas believe that if any of the bamboos used for constructing the *chaangi* (bamboo made bed like structure to carry the dead) are left over they should not be retained in the house as it is not good for the family. If the cows curl their tails around the bamboo *khuta* in the cowshed, the household may suffer. There is no logic behind these beliefs but these superstitions still prevail.

If in dreams one sees snakes chasing him or her, sees his own house on fire, somebody taking away paddy from the granary, a fallen tooth or nail, dogs moving in a sitting posture, vultures sitting sit on the roof of the household, these are considered bad and dangerous signals. If in dreams, one sees a dead person and gets advice, the advice then should be carried out if possible. If a pregnant woman sees a dead person in her dreams, it is believed that that person is being reborn in her womb. If in dreams one sees someone stamping on the *juguli* (cooked rice mixed with *baakhor* for preparing rice beer) then the real taste of the rice beer would not come. If one sees white fish in dreams then he would acquire wealth.[61] While starting on a journey seeing unmarried woman is inauspicious. If one chokes while taking food then it is believed that someone close is remembering him or her, if one chokes while taking betel nuts it is believed that, that person is being discussed.

Status of Women

Traditionally, the role of plains Tiwa woman has been confined to the domestic sphere while the public sphere even to-day remain exclusinely a male domain. The prevalent socio-cultural ethos excludes women from the decision making bodies, making them less able and they are denied equal opportunities strengthened by the values embodied in patriarchy. But though the plains Tiwa society is patrilineal where heredity and inheritance is traced through the father, women in Tiwa society enjoy a position of respect and grace, there being no domination of one sex over the other unlike the pan Indian scenario. Both the sexes contribute towards a cohesive social life. Dowry, divorce, wife beating is almost unheard of. In the domestic and household affairs, women play a prominent role and the responsibilities of bringing up the children lie with them. Their socio-economic activities include not only looking after the siblings, but cultivation, cattle rearing, weaving, doing even trade. Her work starts from early morning. She would wake up, clean the house, prepare and serve meals, then set out for agricultural fields for transplantation of seedlings and harvesting. She is also engaged in rearing pigeons, ducks, and chicken. She also rears *eri* and weaves *endi* shawl and all cotton clothes like *gamocha* (towel), *chador*, bedsheet etc. She sells pigeons, cocks, ducks, etc. and by selling them earns money to buy the essential commodities of the household or her necessities. There are times when she engages in mud plastering of the walls of her house. The Plains Tiwa women do not take rice beer. On the whole, women are more laborious than men. The religious and secular powers are however vested with the male members of the society with the exception of *haari kunwari*.

Village Organisation (Hill Tiwas)

The organisation of a village in the hill areas of Karbi-Anglong differs. In the hill areas there is a chief called *Loro* for each region. Under him are the *doloi, pator, hataari, deori, saaot, maaji* and *baarikhaa*. Generally every village headman with the council of elders settles all disputes and problems both social and religious, but when they cannot settle them, they refer them to the regional set up and their orders are to be followed. At present there are ten *Loros* in Hamren division amongst the hill Tiwas and they are Amswoi Loro, Ronghkoi Loro, Amri Loro, Amkha Loro, Magra Loro, Lumphai Loro, Amtong Loro, Saga Loro. Amni Loro. It is only in the main *(pinong)* villages that Loro exists, the branch *(faam holaa)* villages do not have Loro but for the maintenance of law and order, *chaangdoloi*, *chaangmaaji*, *deori*, *haataari*, *surumaa*, *saot* and *baarikhaa* exist.

Chaamaadi or Youth Dormitory

The *chaamaadi* or dormitory of Tiwa boys is generally situated at one end of the village. It acts as a guard house for the villages though no weapons are kept there. The word *chaamaadi* is a combination of two words *chaa* which means boys and *maadi* meaning enjoyment. The physical structure of a *chaamaadi* resembles a large hall and a number of boys sleep there at night. It is constructed about two metres above the ground on wooden posts or stilts. On both sides, the roof slopes down to the level of the floor. The floor is of split bamboo or may be wooden and there is also a fireplace. A notched log is used for gaining access from the ground. There is a ladder on its backside also. The dormitory is open on both ends, so that the view outside is un-impeded.

The floor area of the dormitory consists of four undivided parts each with a specific purpose.[62] The portion in front of the main post is called *numaaji* and is used for various ceremonies of the dormitory. The *nukthi* is the sitting area and contains the fireplace. To the left of the entrance is the *nucha* which is the space used for sleeping purposes and opposite to it is the *nukur* which is used for storing firewood and implements. Three main posts support the roof. The front post is called *bor-jelaa* or elder brother of the dormitory, the central one is called *bor-kabi* or brother-in-law and rear one is called *haarikunwari* or younger sister. The central post or *bor kabi* has a significant role in the functions of the *chaamaadi*. The cross beams of the dormitory are decorated with carvings of animals, birds and female breasts by a person called *khandaar*. A string of bones of sacrificed pigs is kept hanging from the front cross beam on the reverse side. The drums and flutes also are hung on the cross beams in the *chaamaadi*. Women and girls are prohibited from entering the dormitory but may watch the functions from outside.

Normally after six years have passed, a new dormitory is constructed when the summer sowing is complete. The old dormitory is pulled down after a ritual is performed and the construction activity is undertaken by the new entrants to the senior group. This group along with the *chaangdoloi* and the priest go to the forest and select three trees for the main posts of the dormitory. Other materials like bamboo, cane and thatching grass are collected on the same day and brought to the village along with the posts. When construction is complete, two village magicians (*ojhaas*) are the first to enter the new dormitory house. One of them makes a fire outside the dormitory and carries it to the front entrance. Then the other receives the fire from him and formally places it in the fire place.

The following day is celebrated as *kheljaawaa* festival which is usually a Monday. This festival is held once in six years. On this occasion, oblations and prayers are offered to the presiding deities to protect their land, homes and villages. The ritual takes place in the *numaaji* of the dormitory. Five pigs and a number of ducks and fowls are sacrificed. The rest of the flesh is consumed later on.

In the evening, the priest and all the elders assemble in the house of the village chief (*doloi*) to receive the new entrants to the junior group (*khorkia paanthaais*) of the dormitory. The *chaangdoloi*, who is the leader of the dormitory and his deputy go to the house of every eligible boy and brings them all one by one. While collecting the boys from their houses, the *chaangdoloi* and the *chaangmaaji* sing a song explaining the objective of their visit. The mother also accompanies the son to the house of the chief. The procedure may take the whole night if the number of the boys is large.

The leaders of the new dormitory are selected the next day i.e. Tuesday by the priest and the *doloi* in consultation with the *buraakhel*. The new officials must belong to a clan different from that of their respective predecessors. This is to ensure that all clans get representation and justice is meted out. The *chaangmaaji* is selected by the *chaangdoloi* with the consent of the village elders. The other officials are selected by the *chaangdoloi* and the *chaangmaaji* with the consent of the village elders. A feast is arranged in the evening in the dormitory to bid farewell to the outgoing officials of the dormitory. After the feast, the ceremony is over.

The youth dormitory or *chaamaadi* is a very important institution in the hill villages. Unless the boys fall ill, they are to spend all their working and sleeping hours in the dormitory and can visit their homes only for meals. This system is rigidly enforced and non-compliance may result initially in fines and later on in ostracisation of the family.

The parents have no claim to their son once he enters the dormitory. He cannot help his family in agricultural operations except as a member of the *dekaakhel* and does not maintain a separate relationship with them except for taking meals at home. The boys of the dormitory acquire a thorough knowledge of the economic system of the families in the village as they work as its members for each family of the village. The boys of the *chaamaadi* are to obey the orders of the *chaangdoloi* and perform all sorts of work as directed by him. They hoe, level fields of the villagers, sow and reap their paddy, fetch bamboo from the jungle for building houses etc. When a villager wants some work to be done by the dormitory boys, he goes to the *chaangdoloi,* as he is the leader and offers him betel nuts with leaves and traditional beer and asks for help. If it is accepted, help is assured. In the morning, the boys go to work in the fields with beating of drums and singing of songs and work till it gets dark. The singing and beating of drums is a unique activity in the hill villages performed during agricultural operations like sowing and harvesting of paddy to allay their boredom. It is called *dekaajowaa.*[63] At noon, there is an interval during which they take meal provided by the householder for whom they have been working and also take some rest. The officials do not work but play on flutes, drums and sing songs supervising their activities. The boys are paid a nominal sum and the money collected in this manner is deposited with the *chaangdoloi* for six years till the next *kheljaawaa* festival, when it is utilised for buying various articles for the festival as well as salt. The boys go to the *chaamaadi* at dusk and the younger ones duty is to prepare the fireplaces for them. They go to their respective homes only for meals and come back to the *chaamaadi.* When it is time they sleep on the bamboo mats. The boys of the *chaamaadi* also cultivate agricultural land belonging to the *chaamaadi.* When the harvesting of the land is complete, it is stored in a separate granary and is consumed on festive occasions. It may also be given on loan to needy villagers which is returned after the next harvest. If the *chaamaadi* boys work in the house of one of officials for two days they must also work for two days in each of the houses of other officials, such has been the tradition.

Clan

The origin of a person in the hill areas can be traced from the clan (*kul* also called *khul* or *gotra*) to which he belongs. In one clan there may be several sub- clans. According to a legend, the Tíwas divided themselves in five groups at Amswoi, where they stayed for several years after migration from the Jayantia hills[64]. These five divisions arose from the name of the first settlement after they moved in different directions due to differences. These divisions were *Ams-ali, Majrong-ali, Rongkhoi-ali, Amni-ali,* and *Majra-ali*. In one clan, there may be several sub-clans. In one *mohar* (*phoid*), there may be more than one *khul*. For example:-

(1) *Aamsiwaali, Amsongwaali, Amfiwaali* and *Khamliwaali*

(2) *Pumaawaali, Famjongwaali, Mathrangwaali*

(3) *Kholaarwaali, Modarwaali, Madurwaali, Puruwaali* and *Ladurwaali*

(4) *Mithiwaali, Lumphoiwaali*

(5) *Maslaiwaali, Melangwaali, Sagrawaali, Damlongwaali, Aagariwaali*

(6) *Khoraiwaali, Malongwaali, Muniwali, Sugaiwaali*

(7) *Darphangwaali, Dilarwaali, Samsolwaali*

(8) *Markhangwaali*

(9) *Salengwaali, Khajarwaali*

The suffix '*waali*' denotes that the clans are of matrilineal descent. Generally the menfolk while identifying their own *khel* use 'Jelaa'. *Waali* is used for both male female relations[65].

Clans or clusters of clans regulate marriage among the Tiwas. Marriage between the Tiwa clans of the same *mahari* is taboo. If any such marriage takes place severe punishment is given to both the girl and the boy. However, members of a clan may marry each other if they belong to separate *maharis* and live in separate villages. In the same manner, marriage between the members of a clan is permitted provided they stay in different villages and belong to separate clusters. If they belong to the same village, marriage is not permitted. Within the village marriage between the clans of different clusters is possible. But the boy or the girl, as the case may be, must belong to a clan other than that of the mother. The children take the clan of the mother.

The sons of the family do not marry girls belonging to their fathers's clan and the daughters also do not marry boys belonging to their father's clan. A violation of the rule of exogamy is severely dealt with.

Amongst the hill Tiwas, family is matrilineal. The core of the family is the female. A traditional hill Tiwa family comprises of father, mother, unmarried children, a married daughter with her husband who stays in the house as *kabya* or resident son-in-law. The role of the husband in the wife's house is different. He does not interfere in the management of any affairs in family matters. It is the responsibility of the wife's brothers and her uncles to sort it out. However, even in this kind of arrangement, the husband does have economic obligation towards maintenance of his wife and children. The oral tradition reveals that he cannot shed his responsibilities because of his strong attachment to his mother's house. He plays a role where he balances his acts on both the sides. His role as a son, a husband, a father and an uncle is not compromised.

The other noteworthy aspect is that the children belong to the mother and she has the natural claim and jurisdiction over her sons even after their marriage. He belongs to the mother at all times. The traditional practice is such that it is expected that even in case of death, the son should die in his mother's house. Since the son does not get detached from his mother's house, in case of death also the youngest daughter will have to keep the body of the deceased in the house until taken for cremation. Other ceremonies like naming, wedding rites and rituals are also held in the ancestral house. The self acquired property of the son would remain in his mother's house.

Kinship and Kinship Terminology

Kinship forms the basis of social relationship in homogeneous societies. It is a bond of union of one person to another. Some of the Tiwa kinship terminology are as follows[66] :-

English equivalent	*Relationship terms*
Mother	*Maa*
Father	*Faa, Pabaa*
Grandfather	*Aajaa*

English equivalent	*Relationship terms*
Grandmother	*Aabi*
Father's elder brother	*Aayong*
Father's elder brother's wife	*Aayong*
Maternal uncle	*Maamai*
Maternal uncle's wife	*Aani*
Mother's younger sister's husband	*Aasa*
Mother's younger sister	*Aasi*
Father's sister's husband	*Aasa*
Father's sisters	*Aasi*
Son	*Sa*
Daughter	*Sajo*
Son-in-law	*Jawai*
Daughter-in-law	*Pohari*
Nephew	*Pagin*
Niece	*Pagrai*
Elder brother	*Khaai*
Elder sister	*Paai*
Younger brother	*Kojaal*
Younger sister	*Nimao*
Brother-in-law	*Poonsi*
Wife's elder sister	*Namisah*
Wife's brother-in-law	*Saru*
Co-wife	*Sutunee*
Resident son-in-law	*Kabya*
Grandchildren	*Suh-thin*
Friends	*Syar*
Father-in-law	*Huh*
Mother-in-law	*Niv*
You	*Na*
We	*Syang*

Borjelaa

The word *jelaa* in Tiwa dialect refers to masculine sex and *bor* means big or senior. Thus, *borjelaa* is the eldest male in a *vamsa* who is selected for being proficient in traditional rituals.[67] Every family and every clan has a *borjelaa* – while the former has only domestic responsibilities towards his sisters in a hill Tiwa family for solving property disputes or management of the property, etc the latter, has ceremonial and social responsibilities as the male head of the clan to all its members as regards post natal rites and marriage. However, when he cannot be present on certain ceremonial occasions, the *borjelaa* of the family on his behalf carries out the social and ceremonial rites. The *borjela* of the clan is also called *gharbura* and is addressed as *jelaagabi*. His post is hereditary. After his death, his son becomes the *gharbura* or *borjela*. If there is no son, the post goes to the brother of the *gharbura*. He is formally accepted by the village elders in the courtyard of the *borghar*. The *gharbura* may be a married person but must be proficient in the traditional rituals. He has certain restrictions in his diet and movement. Eel and crab are not to be taken by him. He may go to the cremation ground but cannot play active role in the cremation. There is also *sarubura* to assist the *gharbura*. The *gharbura* is the clan guru and the clan gods of the family are worshipped through him. As an elder brother in the sphere of consanguine relationship, he is distinguished by the term *khaai* and in relationship with the descending generation, other than his own children, that is with the children of his sisters and brothers, he is the *mamai* (maternal uncle). The siblings in the lower generation are *paagin* to him.

Borkabir

The *borkabir* in a hill Tiwa family is the husband of the inheritress or younger daughter (*sadya*). He is therefore the youngest brother-in-law. He addresses the *borjela* as *chalarou*. By this term he specifies the *borjelaa* as the elder brother of his wife. Along with the *borjelaa*, he equally shares the responsibility of prayers and worship of the clan gods.

Borhari

The *borhari* is the female counterpart of the *borjelaa* in the level of generation. The word *hari* means the feminine sex and line of descent which when combined with *bor* means the seniormost female collateral in the family. The *borhari* is the mothers eldest sister, immediate or classificatory to the baby. She ratifies every marriage in the bride's house by accepting the formal present of betel nuts and leaves. When the *borjelaa* and *borhari* grow old their functions are conducted by the next junior collateral of the same generation in the order of birth. The *borjelaa* and *borhari* are the senior most members in the clan.

Rites and Rituals (Hill Tiwas)

Birth

In the hill villages and foot hill areas the Tiwas observe a birth ceremony after the naval chord of the child has fallen off and for this ceremony the *jelaas* of the *khel* are invited[67]. The *jelaa* of the *nubaar* sacrifices six pairs of chicken if the baby is a boy and three pairs if the baby is a girl on twenty one banana leaves[68]. According to the custom of the concerned *khel,* the sacrifice and number of leaves vary. After the sacrifice is over, water mixed with *aaroi* rice grains, basil leaves, *dubari* grass is sprinkled to purify and remove uncleanliness. The invited guests are treated with cooked flesh of the sacrificed birds with a lot of pepper and *arum* leaves, There are two *giyaatis* of the *khel* who are selected. The *giyaatis* advise the neonates to obey their parents[69]. The neonates are held by the *giyaatis* and by putting them up and down seven times give them names. By whichever name the baby does not cry, that name is retained. If the baby cries, then another name is uttered and the baby is placed up and down. After the name giving ceremony is over, the assembled people sing *La Li Hillali* together, which differs from the way the plains Tiwas dance.

Marriage

Among the hill Tiwas no marriage can take place in the same *khul*. So after marriage, the man does not identify himself as belonging to his wife's *khul* and vice versa. There are three systems by which a marriage can take place in hill Tiwa society marriage through negotiation, by natural consent and marriage by force[70].

Firstly, if there is an understanding between a girl and a boy then the girl is taken secretly to the boys home and they are made to stay in the boy's home as husband and wife. Later on under the *borjela - kabi's* direction the boy's family go to the girl's house to notify them and the day for marriage is fixed up for them. On that particular day the bride groom and bride under the leadership of the *borjelaa* go to the bride's residence and get married according to the customs prevalent. It is to be noted that as the girl has been taken as daughter-in-law, the mother of the bride receives a certain amount from the bridegroom which is called bride price.

Secondly, after courtship when the boy and the girl enter into a love relationship for a long time, they spend one night at the girl's house sleeping together. The next day it is declared in presence of the *borjelaa* of the girl's family to the elderly people in the village that the boy had come as *kabya* or *gobhia* and the chiefs are treated with rice beer and other delicacies to get social recognition. At a later period one day the bridegroom and the bride go to the groom's residence and pay respects to the parents and others in the family and return to the bride's residence.

The third kind is marriage by force. The love relationship which goes on between a girl and a boy is taken notice of by the youths of the village. If the boy declines to go to the girl's house as *kabya* (*gobhia*) after he enters into a love relationship, then the youths of the village seize an opportunity and forcibly take the boy to the girl's house. They are then made to sit together and by observing the necessary customs and rituals in presence of *borjelaa* the boy takes an oath and after the declaration as husband and wife they are left to live together. The next day the news is given to the boy's home about the marriage and necessary formalities are observed. The hill Tiwa women do not apply *sindur* or vermillion after marriage.

Death

Both cremation and burial are prevalent amongst the hill Tiwas. The hill Tiwas do not keep the dead body for a long time. One of the family members of the deceased goes and conveys the news to the *chaamaadi* in the village with bottles of liquor and he also informs the village headman. Then the villagers assemble. The head of the family is asked if the body is to be buried or cremated and he takes a decision on the basis of his economic condition. If the dead body is to be buried which is called *Sepaat Thuwa* then, a grave is dug, which has to be seven to nine feet long according to clan affiliation and two to three feet wide. The dead body is naked except for a small cloth to cover the private parts and is placed in the grave with leaves and grass underneath. The front portion of the body has to be placed in a northerly direction while the head has to be placed in a north eastern direction. On top of the body, grass, leaves, earth are placed by relatives and friends. Big and small stones are also added on top.

Both plains and hill Tiwas have cremation grounds in their villages and each clan has its own specific area. If a body has to be cremated some of the villagers go to the cremation ground of the village. The women arrange offering for the dead – egg, cakes, rice and liquor. The articles are kept on a banana leaf and two women belonging to different clan of the deceased carry this. The members carry straw for lighting and take with them rice and egg. On the way to the cremation ground they leave marks of rice grains on the way. Firewood is collected from nearby jungle. Women including the kith and kin of the deceased go ahead of the bier carrying the body and sing good deeds of the dead and also sing songs of lamentation. Four persons carry the bier. The pall bearers are generally the relatives of the deceased. When they have to cross a channel or stream, the women would place a thread over it so that the spirit may also cross over. Before proceeding to the cremation ground, with the body, they place ash on the front side of the house which they cover with a bamboo basket so that nobody should enter from that side for some time. When the funeral procession reaches the cremation ground, a funeral pyre is made with seven layers of firewood on it. Above the stocks of firewood is placed the bier with the body on it, the body facing the house of the deceased in an east-west direction with head pointing to the east. Before the body is placed on the platform, liquor is poured on the mouth of the deceased, offerings brought by the women are made and betel nut is offered. First the relations of the deceased place firewood followed by others. The son of the deceased goes seven times around the body and then applies fire to the mouth of the deceased and if there is no son a kin applies fire.[71] If the body burns easily it is a good sign for that family. If the fire does not burn easily the Tiwas believe that the dead man must have had hopes to eat something and hence food is given. If the right leg rises in an upward direction it is considered ill for the family and if the left leg rises up it is considered ill for the clan as a whole. There are many traditional beliefs regarding the dead in hill Tiwa Society too.

When the funeral party returns to the house, they are sprinkled with water mixed with basil leaves, gold and silver ornaments as a purificatory ritual, The pall bearers are also purified with flowers. There is no feast on the occasion of the death ceremony.

Khari swa or Karam

The hill Tiwas do not have the custom of observing death ceremonles separately for every deceased member either for *sraddha* or *doha*[72]. In a particular *vamsa* in a year for the upliftment of the souls of the deceased members, a function is held jointly in the *nubaar* (*barghar*) in which all members are expected to contribute towards the expenses. The invited guests of the *khel* and the kith and kin of the deceased members pray for the departed souls and offer beer meat and rice. It is to be noted that when meat is offered to the deceased members, it is to be cooked in bamboo *chunga* devoid of oil, salt, turmeric and chilly. It is the custom to offer the deceased members such food by the *barjela* by observing necessary customs. After the offerings are made to the departed souls, the food is taken and kept in the banks of streams.

Property Rights and Inheritance

The heredity and mode of inheritance is matrilineal in hill Tiwa villages. From oral tradition, customary laws and age old practices, the ancestral land in hill Tiwa villages would pass over from the mother to the youngest daughter called *sadya*. The youngest daughter is to remain in the mother's house and the ancestral property would be handed over to her with certain liabilities and obligations. The youngest daughter however has no authority over the family wealth and property and therefore cannot sell or dispose any part of them at her will and pleasure. She is just the custodian of the property. The real control is in the hands of her maternal uncle. The other daughters in the family may stay in the same village in separate and new houses which are generally constructed with the material assistance of their parents and they also get a share of the paddy lands owned by their parents, though the youngest daughter (*sadya*), gets the biggest share. The sons in the family go out to other families to serve as *kabya* and do not get right to inherit their parents property. In case of the death of the youngest daughter, the ancestral property would pass over to the next youngest in line. These days in some families, the son with his wife as well as one of the daughters with her husband live in the parental home after marriage.

Titles

The Hill Tiwas have surnames like Amsi, Maslai, Kholar, Lumphui, Hukai, Mador, Phamjong, Pumah etc.

Status of Women

As stated earlier, the hill Tiwa society is matrilineal and the status accorded to women is an institutionalized part of their social structure. Heredity and inheritance is traced through the mother, but the religious and secular powers are vested with the male with the exception of *haari*. Even in the political arena, women are excluded. In the administration of the village there is no place for the customary laws that are in operation according to oral tradition state that ancestral land would pass over from the mother to the youngest daughter whom they call *Sadya*. But though it appears that women are bestowed with a lot of rights and privileges, in reality the hill Tiwa women cannot do anything without the consent and approval of the menfolk, particularly, the maternal uncle and the brothers. Women cannot even enter the *chaamaadi* but can watch functions from outside. Women's activities relate to the socio-economic domain. Their contribution to the social development of the society is immense. Hill Tiwa women are also more laborious than their male counterparts. They take with them *dao* in their hands and axe on their shoulders and go to cut grass, do hoeing and plant seedlings by jhum cultivation which is practised in the hills, along with their male counterparts. They wake up early in the morning around three to prepare the morning meal and the mid-day meals. Thereafter they set out to work in the agricultural fields. They rear pigs and chicken. They weave clothes for themselves as well as for the menfolk with beautiful designs. They can also weave in *maatir saal*, in which they put threads around the waist. They are also adept in the art of dyeing, by taking out the juice from different seeds or fruits like *kehraj*, *silikha*, *kendugan*, lac etc. They also engage themselves in harvesting, threshing, de-husking of paddy. Hill Tiwa women take rice beer occasionally and say that it relieves their monotony. They can be seen taking the *kho* (basket) on their backs laden with, ginger, turmeric, corn, chillis, pine-apples and walking several miles to sell their home grown products. Like their male counterparts they too come a long way with baskets on their backs to sell or exchange goods in the annual *Joon Beel Mela* which is held near Jagiroad.

Language and Literature

Dwan which is the mother tongue of the Tiwas bears similarity to Bodo, Dimasa, Tipra, and Garo but has no script. It has not yet attained the status of language. It is a branch of Boro language of the Sino-Tibetan speech family.

Most of the educated plains Tiwa men pen down their thoughts in Assamese while the hill Tiwa people prefer to express themselves in Dwan. A few books which have been published by the Tiwas show that both Assamese and Roman scripts have been used. But majority of the works are in Assamese script. Reverend M. Balwan has written *Outline of Lalung Grammar*, *Tiwa Maat, Lalung Dictionary, Sikai*, *Pihini Pihini Khorong*. All these works belong to the sixties and the early seventies. The prominent Tiwa writers using Assamese script are late Ganesh Senapati, Moneswar Deori, Late Lalit Bharali, Bolai Ram Senapati etc. The *Tiwa Mathonlai Tokhra* is their literary forum and they hold their annual sessions at different places in Assam. They have a number of journals, prominent among them being *Ringsaang* (Assamese script), *Thuraang* (Assamese script), *Thuri*, the contents are written in *Dwan* (Tiwa dialect) using Roman script. Late Lalit Bharali had attempted and started writing an Assamese-Tiwa dictionary, but because of his untimely death the work remained incomplete.

As mentioned earlier, the plains Tiwas have been influenced by Assamese so much that they have almost forgotten their own dialect.

The hill Tiwas on the other hand speak their own dialect. They find it difficult to speak and pronounce the fourth consonant of every line of Assamese alphabets. Thus, *gha, jha, dha, bha*, is pronounced in a different way by the hill Tiwas[73]. Hence there are differences in pronunciation between hill Tiwas and plains Tiwas. This can be seen below:

Hill Tiwa Pronunciation	Plains Tiwa Pronunciation	English Meaning
gohor, gor	*ghar,*	house, home
dohoriboloi	*dhoriboloi*	to catch
kura	*ghura*	horse
daan or taan	*dhan*	paddy
baat or bahaat	*bhaat,*	cooked rice

The hill Tiwas cannot pronounce the *pratham 'cha'* and *ditiya cha* of Assamese alphabets well, but the plains Tiwas can pronounce the '*ja*' or *pratham cha* of Assamese alphabets. The following are examples[74]:

Hill Tiwa Pronunciation	Plains Tiwa Pronunciation	English Meaning
Sokha	*Jokha*	small
Sing	*Jing*	we
Saar	*Saar/jaar*	who
Sakhala	*jakhala*	when
Sa'ri	*Sari*	four

Even in the Assamese consonants of *ka, ta* and *pa*, in the first and third *barna* there is a difference between the hill Tiwa and the plains Tiwa pronunciation. The examples are[75]:

Hill Tiwa pronunciation	Plains Tiwa pronunciation	English Meaning
Poonsi	*Boonsi*	Brother-in-law
Koi	*Goi*	Betel nuts
Torga	*Dorga*	Door

Like Assamese language, the Tiwa dialect also has some words a part of which is repeated, examples of which are given:

Tiwa	*Assamese*	*English Meaning*
Keet-naad	*Geet maat*	Songs
Khul-bangsa	*Kul-bangsa*	Clan-lineage
Pol-pudi	*bol-budhi*	Strength, intelligence
Mis-maasu	*Goru-moh*	Cow-buffaloes

In Tiwa dialect there is use of singular and plural. When a singular word becomes plural *rou* or *rao, geda* and *boor* is added at the end of the word[76]. In case of numericals *boor*, *rou, rao* and *geda* are not used.

Linga (gender)

In Tiwa dialect there are four kinds of *linga* (gender)- *pulinga, strilinga*, *ubhaylinga* and *klibalinga*[77]. The word at the end indicates male or female. Generally, *mewa, moswa, sa* is used to indicate male while *sajo, magri, musulung* is added at the end indicate female gender[78]. For example:-

Ubhaylinga	Pulinga	Strilinga
libing	*mewa libing*	*margi libing*
people	male	female
korkha (child)	*korkha sa* (boy)	*korkha sajo* (girl)
tu (bird)	*moswa tu* (male bird)	*muslung tu* (female bird)

The Tiwa dialect has adjectives like *nithaawaa* which means beautiful, *thaaw* meaning sweet, *khedang* meaning raw, *kojaa* meaning red etc.

Counting of Numbers

In Tiwa dialect, higher numbers are counted by twenties.[80] While counting figures they start from one (*kisa*) to twenty (*ekhuri*) and thereafter add one, two, three to the twenty (*ekhuri*). The counting of numbers goes like this:-

Tiwa	*English*
Kisa	one
Kinning	two
Theen	three
Saari	four
Paas	five
Siu	six
Saat	seven
Aat	eight
Nou	nine
Toh	ten
Egaaro	eleven
Baaro	twelve
Thero	thirteen
Suida	fourteen
Phondra	fifteen
Sollo	sixteen
Sathara	seventeen
Athaaro	eighteen
Unnees	nineteen
Ekhuri	twenty
Ekhuri kisa	twenty one
Ekhuri kinning	twenty two
Ekhuri theen	twenty three
Tikhuri	means two *(khuri)* equivalent to forty
Tikhuri kisa	Forty one
Tikhuri kinning	Forty two
Theen khuri	three twenty's *(khuri)* which is equal to sixty

Similarly *Theen kuri kisa* means sixty one, *thzeen* meaning three, *khuri* means twenty and *kisa* means one.

Saree khuri	means four twenty's which is equal to eighty
Paas khuri or	means five twenty's which
So'sa	is equal to 100
Sosa kisa	which means one hundred and one
Sosa ekhuri kisa	means one hundred twenty one
Ta sa or *haazaar sa*	means ten hundred or one thousand

Idioms and Proverbs

In most languages, including Tiwa dialect maxims also called idioms exist. The formation of such maxims is a rather difficult procedure. Some particular words are combined with others to form a meaning[81].

Every aspect of the Tiwa dialect has not been mentioned here but only a bird's eye view has been presented.

NOTES AND REFERENCES

1. Giddings Cf V.B. Sachdeva. *An Introduction to Sociology*, Allahabad, 1984, p. 56.
2. *Ibid*, p.57.
3. *Ibid.*
4. Field Study.
5. Field Study.
6. RRK, p.72.
7. *Ibid.*
8. *Ibid.*
9. *Ibid.*
10. *Ibid.*
11. *Ibid.*

12. LA, p. 23.
13. Deori M., *Tiwa Samaj*, Jorhat, 1983, p.77 (henceforth TS).
14. *Ibid.*
15. *Ibid.*
16. LA, p. 37.
17. Choudhury, N.K. and M.M. Das, *The Lalung Society*, Kolkata, 1974, p.,63 (henceforth LSCD).
18. *Ibid.*, p.,60.
19. *Ibid.*, p.,59.
20. *Ibid.*, p.,58.
21. *Ibid.*, p.,60.
22. *Ibid.*
23. *Ibid.*
24. LST, p.,65.
25. *Ibid*, p.,65.
26. *Ibid*, p.,70.
27. *Ibid.*
28. *Ibid*, p.,68.
29. LA, p.,55.
30. T.S., p.,63.
31. LA, p.,56.
32. *Ibid*, p.,57.
33. T.S. p.,66.
34. *Ibid.*
35. *Ibid,* p.,67.
36. *Ibid.*
37. *Ibid*, p., 68.
38. LA, p., 58.
39. Deori, M. *Morigaon Jilar Lokasmriti,* Morigaon, 1994, p.76 (henceforth MJL).

40. *Ibid.*, p.76.
41. LST, p. 42.
42. *Ibid.*
43. MJL, p.77.
44. TS, p. 56.
45. *Ibid.*
46. *Ibid.*, p.57.
47. *Ibid.*, p.60.
48. LST, p.5.
49. *Ibid*, p.71.
50. TS, p.69.
51. Senapati, G.C., *'Tiwa Jaatir maangkhor sthaapon aaru sa daah prothaa'* in *Rinchaang,* second issue, 1973-74, p.198.
52. *Ibid*, p.200.
53. *Ibid.*
54. *Ibid.*
55. LST. p.55.
56. Senapati, G.C., loc.cit, p.203.
57. *Ibid*, p.201.
58. TS, p.73.
59. Senapati, G.C., loc.cit, p.203.
60. LST. p.61.
61. *Ibid.*
62. TS, p.103.
63. Gohain, B.K., *The Hill Lalungs*, Guwahati, 1992, p.29 (henceforth HLG).
64. *Ibid*, p.28.
65. LA, p.36.
66. Field Study, Informant Rimol Amsih.
67. Field Study.

68. Senapati, G.C., *Tiwa Samaajor ahaus bidhi in Ringsang* First issue, 1972-73, p.111.
69. *Ibid.*
70. TS, p. 67.
71. Senapati, G.C., loc.cit, p.111.
72. Field Study, also see HLG, p.43.
73. Field Study.
74. Field Study.
75. TSRG, Part I, p.50.
76. *Ibid,* pp.51-52.
77. *Ibid*, p.52.
78. TS, p.104.
79. *Ibid.*
80. *Ibid*, p.108.
81. RRK, pp.83-84.

3

Economy

All over the world, human beings are engaged in economic activities for sustenance. The range of economic activities are wide and differ from place to place and area to area. Cities and towns, urban and rural divides no doubt exist, yet most conscious human beings are engaged in some economic activity or the other. Being inhabitants of an agrarian country, the Tiwas both plains and hills, who are mainly rural based have an agrarian economy. Agriculture is their chief occupation and principal means of livelihood. There are however some ecological variations between those living in the hills and those in the plains. Their economy is supplemented with other forms of vocations like spinning and weaving, fishing, piggery, poultry and cattle, arts and crafts. In order to survive they have learned the hard way of adapting themselves to their environment. Educated Tiwas engaged in governmental jobs, corporate sector etc. are few and far between. The literacy rate is quite low as Tiwa families require their family members to help in the fields. However, they may still boast of their men engaged in professions like teaching, medicine and administration. In a recent census done voluntarily by the Assam Tiwa Students Union in the proposed Autonomous District, the Tiwa literacy rate was shown as 21%.[1] The percentage of Tiwas engaged as cultivators is shown as 92.7%, official workers shown as 5.6% and others as 2.7% in a total Tiwa population of 3,16,949 persons, in an area of 3294 sq. km.[2]

The Tiwas are self sufficient in basic needs- food, shelter and partly clothing. For basic necessities, the village is a self contained productive unit and production activities are arranged by each family either on its own or with the help of hired labour or by the corporate system of labour called *haadaari* which is a system of reciprocal help.

Plains Tiwas

Agriculture

As stated earlier, agriculture is the main occupation of the plains Tiwas and rice is the principal crop. It keeps them engaged for almost nine months of a year beginning with the onset of pre-monsoon showers in the end of March or in early April. M. Deori writes that "the Tiwas observe three main ceremonies in respect of agriculture at different seasons of the year and offer *pujaa* to different gods."[3] At first they observe *jong khong pujaa* and before this *pujaa* is observed, nobody should go to the fields for cultivation. Then they observe *aarkura* or *aarkota* festival after which the jungles are cut and cleaned and made ready for cultivation. In the third phase they perform Lakhshmi *pujaa*. The Tiwas believe that *Mahadeo Gossain* first created the cultivator and it was on his directions that *Chaaribhai-Chaarikora* (deity of four brothers, Laamkaa Raja, Gurupaar, Daseniri and Rajeniri) but now considered as a single deity imparted the knowledge of cultivation to men.[4] *Saali* variety which they call *haali*, (*ha* meaning land and *li* meaning wide) is the major crop of the plains Tiwas. *Aahu* and *baao* varieties of paddy are also grown. Cash crops, such as vegetables, fruits, coconuts, areca nuts, sesame, mustard, arum, turmeric, ginger, etc are generally cultivated on homestead lands by individual families.

For cultivation of paddy, land is ploughed during the wet months between April and September. On the first April shower, a summer variety of paddy called *aahu* is sown which takes about three to four months to ripen. The *aahu* paddy is cultivated in low-lying lands and thrives on pre-monsoon rains. After harvesting is complete the land is not utilized for any other crop till the next *aahu* season. *Baao,* is another variety of summer paddy grown on lands where inundation occurs during monsoon. This variety is rather sturdy as it grows fast even if the level of water goes up. Both *aahu* and *baao* varieties are not cultivated extensively. *Saali* is the principal winter crop. Its cultivation is comparatively a long process.

As stated above, the Tiwas begin their agriculture operation in the month of April customarily after the *jongkhong* festival. Manure is applied to the fields in the months of February and March. Majority of the Tiwas depend upon local cowdung as manure and only a few persons apply chemical fertilizer and pesticides.[5] Cowdung is stored in a pit near the cowshed and is carried to the fields in bullock carts or in shoulder load baskets.

In the fields, the manure is kept in small heaps. The early monsoon in April/May distributes this manure throughout the field. During the first ploughing which is generally done by bullocks, furrows are made in the fields. A second and third ploughing with an interval of ten to twenty days between each ploughing is done for regular plots and levelled. After the second ploughing, the seedbed is made ready for sowing. Sometimes, a small plot of land near the homestead is tilled and used for sowing. For sowing, an auspicious date is fixed. Prior to that, the seeds are taken out from the store house and processed in water. The seeds are carried to the seedbed on the pre-fixed day by the *gharburaa* or head of the family and distributed. A scarecrow is fixed in the centre of the seedbed in order to scare away the birds.

There are certain, beliefs amongst the plains Tiwas in respect of paddy cultivation. They believe that sowing of seeds should begin on a Monday while harvesting should begin on a Wednesday.[6] A ceremony known as *dhaanar muthi lowaa* is observed at the time of sowing at individual households.[7] The *haari kunwari* would clean the house early in the morning on that particular day and near the *thuna khuta* of the *barghar* a tray containing paddy seeds and a bowl containing rice powder, leaves of *banamaalaa* and water are kept. After offering a prayer the *gharburaa* sacrifices a fowl or a small chicken over the mixture of rice powder, *banamaalaa* and water. The blood of the sacrificed bird is smeared on the *thuna khuta*. The *gharburaa* takes the seeds kept near the *thuna khuta* and goes to the field and spreads those in the field, at first with his left hand and then with right hand. Sometimes, other villagers or neighbours are also invited to plough the field. This ceremony is used to designate someone as *borjelaa*[8]. In a jovial manner his hands are tied to the back and he is required to proceed to the house which has arranged the ceremony. He goes to the *barghar* and sits till the family members receive him with due honour. He is honoured with a chicken and a pot of traditional beer. At noon a feast is arranged. While partaking food a concoction of *banamaalaa* leaves, water and rice powder is sprinkled over them.

The Tiwas believe that the mixture is the boon given by goddess Lakshmi.[9]

In the plains, paddy is not directly sown in the land from where it is harvested. According to the procedure, after the seedling attains a height of about one foot which generally takes a month, they are transplanted. Transplantation of seedlings is undertaken between July and September for *Saali* paddy, during the period of heavy rains. A day prior to transplantation, the seedlings are pulled out from the seedbed in the evening and kept in the open in the courtyard for the night. This task is performed by men. Since the seedlings are pulled out they have to be planted before the sun reaches its zenith, otherwise they do not take root. Transplantation is generally done by women. Since transplantation has to be completed within a short time in the early hours of the morning, help is sought by various families for additional working hands. This is rendered by the *haadaari khel* (a voluntary group of girls or women or men) arranged by the *chaangdoloi* a day ahead. This group is constituted for a specific piece of work. The *haadaari khel* or a number of women assemble in the house of the family on whose field the seedlings are to be transplanted and at sunrise proceed to the field along with the rice saplings. Older men accompany to offer required help and also to supervise that everything goes on well. The seedlings are placed at equal distance in a line from one side about nine inches apart from one another. Two or three saplings are put together at each of the places. After the work has been completed, the women return to the place, where they had assembled in the morning and are given food. Weeding is generally undertaken by men.

The crop is ready for harvesting in the months of November and December. Harvesting is undertaken both by men and women, though women generally reap the crop and men join if the field is large. It starts on an auspicious pre-fixed day and the first bundle is carried home on the same day. The first crop i.e., *Lakshmi* is welcome in the home with a song called *Aahoi Lowaa.*[10] On the first day of harvesting the Tiwa cultivators take bath, wear clean clothes, take a banana leaf (front portion) and a new piece of cloth and gets hold of a bunch of ripe paddy. After three bunches of paddy are cut, the first bunch is wrapped in the banana leaf and put on the head and without talking to anyone and without looking back the person proceeds to his home and keeps it in the walls of the home granary carefully.[11] In some villages, the person who first cut the ripe paddy cuts nine bunches in the name of nine plants and wraps the nine bunches in new cloth.[12] These bunches are placed on the head of one of the male family members and taken home without speaking a word to anyone on the way. On the last day of harvesting the relatives and neighbours also assist the individual households. On the last day also nine bunches of ripe paddy are carried on the head and tied to a betel nut tree at home. On *Maakh Bisu* day with incense sticks and *dhunaa*, the bunches are hung on the walls of the granary. A feast is arranged on that day itself or a month later where the villagers who took part in the harvesting are invited. *Zu* is also arranged. This is called *Naraa Chigaa Khowaa.*[13] For purposes of harvesting also, additional hands are required and this help is obtained from hired labour or *haadaari khel*. On the day of harvesting, each woman-member of the group carries with her sufficient quantity of uncooked rice and her own sickle. This being the lean season before the harvest, the family for whom the haadaari is working is not expected to contribute anything. The uncooked items are then all put together and cooked for consumption and taken by all in an interval as harvesting is a day-long operation. The stalks of paddy are cut with sickles about nine centimeters from the ground and bundles are made, each weighing about twenty kg. These bundles are tied with wisps of hay and carried by family members or the *deka khel* members if help was sought. One bundle each is tied at each end of a *biriyaa* (bamboo pole placed across the shoulder) and taken home and is stored in the granary. The Tiwas still believe that originally all the food grains were submerged in the ocean and were brought out on land by their forefathers who appeased the goddess of agriculture through prayers and sacrifices. Before harvesting operations begin, ritualistic prayers are offered to Lakshmi. The song sung in praise of Lakshmi is called the harvesting song by the Tiwas. It goes like this-

'O' ai Lakshmi tutui sagarniaai, dhop khelai thab
Abo' sananae sang rubanae sang
Khejanga foi rangafai

Hash tak takaigara
far kar-kurai gara
Sananae sang, rufanae sang
Ranjana fai

The English meaning is taken from Agnihotri's

O' Mother Lakshmi, come out of the sea!
Offering incense and joss sticks
We kneel before you,
In tender leaves
We place our offerings
And pray in plaintive call
Please graciously accept'em all
Ducks we have offered
Cocks we have offered
In times of trouble
May you shoot the trouble away
May you be seated on these thrones
Of shining silver, shining gold.[10]

Threshing in the plains villages is generally done with the help of a pair of bullocks or cows tied together with loose loops at the end of a rope and making them go over the paddy stalks in the courtyard of the household. The paddy thus gets separated from its stalk and the stalks are removed by fanning.

Husking of paddy is done by women by the *dheki* in the traditional way. The *dheki* is a long and heavy wooden beam fixed with a pestle at one end which when operated at the other end by one foot would go up and down to the mortar and its continuity helps in the separation of the chaff from the grain.

In the plains, horticultural cash crops, such as, betel nuts, bananas and seasonal vegetables are grown on homestead land. The most important among them is betel nut for which a large area in the backyard is earmarked. Other available spaces are also used to grow the palm but not in the courtyard. The tree begins to yield fruit after almost seven years. It is grown for one's own consumption as well as for earning cash.

Bamboo is another useful commodity which is grown in almost every household. Once grown, it thrives by itself. It is used for multifarious activities. The requirements of a household is generally met from one's own grove, but if additional amount becomes necessary it is obtained from the jungles.

Banana is grown in almost every homestead land. The leaf, fruit and stem of the plant are used for a variety of purposes, besides using them for edible purposes. On ceremonial and formal occasions, cooked food is served on banana leaves. The leaves are also used for packing food to be taken to the fields. The fruit is eaten but more often sold. The pith of the stem is eaten in a variety of ways.

Seasonal vegetables like gourd, arum, legume, egg-plant, pumpkin, cucumber, chillies, sweet potatoes and fruits like papaya, jackfruit, mangoes are grown and sometimes sold. Coconut is also grown as a cash crop. Some families have started growing jute and sugarcane. Jute is a cash crop sold to the traders who come to the village for it. Sugarcane juice is extracted and converted into jaggery and sold in the market. Mustard is grown and used for preparing oil for cooking for domestic consumption.

Rain Making

Whenever the crops are affected by drought, the youths of some villages go from house to house welcome rain by taking the spade, axe, etc. in their hands. They dig the earth in their courtyards by going in a circular manner and sing the welcome rain song which they call *noka kit*.[15] The lady of the household sprinkles water on the youths and makes the courtyard muddy. The *noka kit* is sung accompanied by a special indigenous musical instrument called *uraal*. This instrument is made from a wooden husking pot called *uraal*, a rope and weight. This pot is placed on a bamboo mat. When water is poured into it and the rope is pulled it makes a sound akin to that of rain and thunder. A song accompanies this music, a part of which is given below,

Samdeo, Hajodeo, nokha manae
Khaulo Kaithang
AU !...........ree nakh manae kha
nokha patai labia gaitho
raija norka tha.........
Ramdeo, Hajodeo, Nakhapalai labia gaitho
raija norka tha
Makhinae Kiri Sangai Kiri
Nokha palai laba
Nokha palai labia gaitha
raijae norkha tha..........'

The English translation goes like this

'O God Varuna, the custodian of earth,
Bless us with the showers first,
For without them shall we all
Dwell for sure in hell and fall.'[16]

From area to area the manner in which rain is welcomed differs. In some plains villages in times of drought the young boys get together and go to someones house at night quietly and steals the '*dheki*' (a long wooden beam with a pestle at one end used for grinding purposes, separating grain from chaff etc.) and places it in the *tini-ali* (where three roads meet). Sometimes a water container is placed upside down and other things are also performed in a topsy-turvy manner. When the mistress of the household sees, she vents out her ire. If the wrath and expression are strong the rains come early such is the folk belief of the Tiwas.[17]

Frog Wedding

In some plains Tiwa villages, village girls get hold of two frogs and get them married in the hope of getting rain. They keep the frogs tied together by applying oil and vermillion for four days.[18] Sometimes one may die, in that case the wedding is postponed. But if everything goes on well, then a marriage date is fixed. A fire is lit in the *naamghar* solemnizing the marriage and a feast is arranged. Both groom and brides party observe necessary customs. Sometimes however when there is excessive rainfall and rains do not cease, then the Tiwa people place a bamboo stick with a chilli stuck to it in a water logged area in the belief that rains would cease and people would get respite and relief. They also believe that if people slip and fall with face upwards towards the sky, then the rains would cease. If flowering of mango trees is excessive, it is believed by the Tiwas that there will be storms.[19]

Agricultural Implements

The most important of all the agricultural implements used by the plains Tiwas is the plough (*nangal*). It consists of a beam, a yoke and the body. The yoke rests on the necks of two bullocks. The outer end of the beam is fixed to the middle portion of the body. An iron share is fixed in the anterior end of the body. As the bullocks keep moving the sharp iron share digs the earth and loosens the soil. They also use a harrow (*juwali*) in their fields which resembles a ladder. The length of the *juwali* is about 1.5 metre and the breadth is about 30 cm. A beam is tied to its centre and the other end of the beam is tied to the center of the yoke. The man behind the plough stands on the ladder and it is pulled by the bullocks. Other agricultural implements used are spade, ploughshare, *salmari* (sharp edged instrument), *kanchi (sickle), biriya* (a split bamboo for carrying loads on the shoulder), *dilabari (axle*), *daali* (basket) etc.[20] For dehusking paddy they use *dheki* as mentioned earlier.

Haadaari Khel

In the plains villages, *haadaari khel* system of both males and females exist. *Haadaari khel* is a non formal group of girls and women or men who help in agricultural operation on reciprocal basis. They do not constitute any formal organisation. The assistance of the *haadaari khel* is generally sought in agricultural operation like sowing, transplanting and harvesting of paddy, for mud plastering of walls of new houses etc. On each occasion a group is constituted by the *chaangdoloi* himself on receiving a request from a household. Young girls are selected from houses where they are comparatively free from domestic duties and the work is divided equally among them.

During such times, a senior member of the household remains with the *haadaari khel*. Although the *haadaari khel* is organised on a voluntary basis, help is normally not refused due to social and economic reasons or for ostracisation.

Fishing

Apart from agriculture the plains Tiwas indulge in fishing and this is more particularly done during the monsoon. Fish is an important part of their meals and acts as an appetiser whether fresh or dried. It is eaten in a variety of ways and is considered a delicacy. Although both men and women take part in fishing, for men it is only a pastime whereas for women it is an important domestic economic activity. Fishing implements are made from bamboo by men but they are suitable only for shallow stagnant waters. Otherwise fishing nets are used. Some of the fishing implements used in the plains are *chepaa, polo, jaakoi, dingori, tek, khaaloi, paauri.* The *chepaa* is shaped like a barrel having a closed end while the *polo* resembles a clove with an open circular, opening at the top. The former is used for fishing in shallow running water while the latter is used in shallow stagnant water. Women use *jaakoi* (bamboo made, conical in shape with a big triangular opening). It is pushed into water, kept there for some time and then taken out to collect the fish which entered. Another way is by attracting them in the night with the help of a torch flame and cutting by a *dao*. On festive occasions, particularly during *Maakh Bisu* there is community fishing and fish thus collected is distributed to each household living in that area. This is done on a fixed date decided by village elders and the *doloi*. The catch is divided equally but the chief (*doloi*) gets an additional share.

Poultry and Cattle

The Tiwas in the plains rear pigs and chicken for sale within the village and also for sacrifice during ceremonial occasions. They earn good income from such sales. These days very few plains Tiwa families rear pigs as it is difficult to manage them. Plains Tiwa women generally keep ducks, fowls and pigeon- mostly for sale. Hen eggs are consumed, kept for hatching and are also used for divination purposes. Through sale of eggs also an income is derived. Care of the poultry is the duty of the housewife. Some plains Tiwas have bullocks and cows which are used for agricultural operations.

Crafts

An important economic activity of the male members in Tiwa villages is basket weaving. Baskets and other articles of everyday use are made of bamboo and cane and are used extensively. While making baskets emphasis is laid on durability. Other items which they make are *japaa* (a suitcase), *peraa* (a big suitcase), *saraai* (traditional plate with stand). They also make and repair boats, spinning wheel out of wood. In '*Barat*' festival they use a variety of masks, which they make themselves. Such activity is generally undertaken in the afternoons after the agricultural season is over.

Spinning and Weaving

Plains Tiwa girls and women are adept in the art of spinning and weaving which is an activity exclusively confined to them. Every house hold possesses a loom which is placed on the front side of the house. Knowledge of weaving is considered as qualification for prospective brides and they are not considered fit for marriage, if they do not know the art of weaving. They weave their own clothes, like *mekhelaa* (woven cloth used for lower portion of body), *chador* (woven cloth used for upper portion of body), *gamocha* (towel) etc. in their looms. These days they prefer mill made yarn and readymade dresses.

Food (Chaura Nunga) in Tiwa Dialect

Rice is the staple food of the plains Tiwas. It is taken three times a day in large quantities. Fish, meat and vegetables are also taken along with rice. In the plains, villagers generally take *poita bhaat* (left soaked overnight in water) as their first meal along with chillies, onion and salt. The next mid-day meal is cooked by the housewife which consist of boiled rice, seasonal vegetables available and fish or meat if available. The third meal is taken during night time. They eat a variety of edible leaves like arum whose stem when cooked is a delicacy. Generally they chew betel nuts and leaves after meals. Some of the elderly male members also have the habit of smoking *biri*. M.Deori[21] writes that not only the Tiwas but most of the tribes eat a number of bitter leaves like *moha neem, baahaakaa, bhui, bhekuri teeta* and *sukutaa teeta* at least two days in a week. He says the Tiwas eat these bitter leaves for good health. *Sukutaa* means leaves of jute plant and these are also dried and kept for use in days of scarcity. Sometimes along with these leaves the liver or fat of the pig is cooked with a lot of chillies and this curry is called *khaalaab*-which is so bitter that it leaves a bad taste in the mouth for quite sometime.[22] Very often he says after taking meals they take something bitter as they feel it is healthy. The Tiwas dry fish in a particular way and store them in slender bamboo containers. This is called *sukuti* or *sukati* and can be preserved for sometime. The dried fish which is also prepared for *Sukuti* but not grounded and kept in the slender bamboo containers are called *aaroiya*.[23] Many varieties of fish namely, *chenapholaa, goroi, sol, saal, boraali, rou, dhekera* are dried and preserved and are taken as a delicacy. They also eat a variety of snacks like *saandoh*, (fried rice powder), *pithaa* (rice cake), *koraai* (fried rice), *cheeara* (flat rice), and a variety of sticky rice called *boraa* and rice cooked on *jorasoru*.[24] These days the Tiwas have started taking tea with milk in it. Other dishes of the Tiwas include green leafy vegetables- *maanimuni, maatikaduri, narasinga, agaora, bhebelilotaa, posolaa.*

Rice beer or beer made from fermented rice is not merely a favourite traditional drink of the Tiwas but is also a sacred libation used to appease Gods and spirits. It is called *sui* or *laupani* by them.[25] M Deori states that there is a story associated with how the drink came into being.[26] It is of frequent use at all socio-religious ceremonies like *karam, manshwaa, ratisewaa, jongkhong, sogra, khaplang rawane, bihu, melaa* and in everyday use. It is taken by only male members in the plains. It is courtesy not to take it straight after it is served. To make this traditional *beer*, *baakhor* (indigenous yeast) is essential. The *baakhor* is made by mixing a variety of leaves like *baahaaka* bitter leaves, *bhekuri teetaa, betai phool, porolaaluti, kothaal* (jackfruit) leaves, *kuhiaar* (sugarcane) leaves alongwith a quantity of *aaroi* rice. To this is added an old *baakhor* and all these are ground together in the *dheki*. When it is finely ground it is mixed with rice powder and shaped in a circular way and dried in the sun and then hung in the kitchen walls. If old *(baakhor)* is not added the new (*baakhor*) cannot be prepared. To make the beer, *akaari rice* grains, i.e. those which are broken and could not be cleaned well are required. They are taken and boiled in a vessel with water.[27] When it is half cooked the fire underneath is put out so that the rice becomes hard. Moneswar Deori writes that when the rice is half cooked and strained the beer would taste good.[28] When the cooked rice gets cold, banana leaves are brought and in it are placed the hard solid rice and broken. After this according to the quantity of rice, one, two or half a *baakhor* is added and mixed thoroughly. Rice mixed with *baakhor* is called *juguli* by the Tiwas. It is then covered with banana leaves and over it is placed a burnt cinder, a sickle and a knife. If this is done then it is believed that dead men cannot touch the prepared beer. After keeping for two to three days a fermented smell would pervade. Then two or three litres of water are poured in it. Again after three or four days a little water is added and mixed together with hand. After one or one and a half hours a sieve is taken and the beer is filtered out. The first part of the filtered drink is rather strong and is called *pohon mod.*[30] When water is added to this *juguli* i.e the portion that remains in the pitcher it is less strong and is therefore called *dhoraburhi* or *poniyaa mod.*[31] In Tiwa religious ceremony sacrificial offerings must constitute some quantities of rice beer. There is no better way of keeping the souls of the dead happy and contented than to offer rice beer to them.

Household Utensils

The household utensils of the plains Tiwa comprise of bamboo made articles like *dolaa* (circular shallow container generally used to clean rice), *chaaloni* (similar to *dolaa* with smaller holes at the bottom, through which unwanted parts are removed), *phaashi* (bamboo basket), *khoraahi* (bamboo made round object), *chaakoni* (bamboo made sieve used for filtering traditional rice beer), *thulaa* is used for drinking rice beer.[32] It is made from banana trunk for temporary use when a large number of people are to be served rice beer in festive occasion or *pujaas*. *Jootha jooma lao* is also used for serving rice beer on certain occasions. This is made from *lao* (gourd), a vegetable which has pointed neck. A little of the pointed part is cut and alkali with salt is put into it which destroys the inner fleshy portion. It is then cleaned well, dried and is used to serve rice beer. These days most of the Tiwas purchase kettle, cooking pot, *kerahi* (to cook vegetables) from the plains traders. They have large earthen pots which are used for brewing beer and the *daaron* (wooden kettle like structure) is used for serving traditional rice beer. In tiwa a dialect, plate is called, *Khargsi*, small container *potathi*, glass-*khusharo*, *Shaakuri-sieve*, *Khaamli* and *tokhna* are served small wooden pieces which are used to sit while partaking food, *Kholosh*-pitcher, *Kuthi*-smaller pitcher knife, *haate*, *tharupore, ton*-are all cooking spoons kilo-hand far, phashi-basket.

Clothing

The plains Tiwa women (*maargi libinge*) wear dresses similar to those worn by other rural Assamese women. Their traditional dress comprises of a *kaasong* (a piece of woven cloth stiched on two sides) tied to the waist by riarra and worn to cover the lower part, a *the nasash* and philinge blouse to cover the upper portion of the body. Some of them wear the jaskal to cover the breasts and in it extends a few inches below the knees. The *naara* is used to tie the *Kaasong* and *joskai* in place of a petticoat. The educated and affluent among them wear the petticoats, brassieres, etc. Young girls wear frocks, *(salwaar kaamij)* ribbons, hairclips, cosmetics. The dress of the menfolk mewaa libinge are similar to those worn by other rural Assamese menfolk. The traditional dress Tiva mens, (*mewaa libinge*) are *Khana* (a strip of cloth of placed between the two legs tied waist to cover private parts, (warst coat) to the plains *taagle*. The elderly people wear *dhotis* while the others wear trousers and shirts purchased from the market. They call shirts as *nimaai sola* and *taglaa* (waistcoat). In winter they use coat, sweater and shawl. *Khonia kapor*, *borkapor* (large coarsely woven cloth etc which) were used in lieu of warm clothes earlier have now-a-days become rare.

In the daily life their titular chiefs whom they address as Rajas wear trousers and shirts but they their traditional dress on specific occasions. The dress of the Raja consists a *munga dhoti*, a *munga chola,* a *munga paaguri* (turban), a cotton *chador,* one silver necklace, two *gaamkhaaru* (bracelets) and two ear-rings *(siha)*. Besides these, the Raja takes two *langkhoi* (sword), one *aaron,* one *bisani* (hand made fan), one *rupar paatra* (silver utensil), one *thona*, and one *nichaan* (flag). These days the titular Rajas wear cotton *dhoti*, a cotton *kurta*, cotton turban and take cotton *chador* or *gamocha* and wear some ornaments.

Ornaments

The plains Tiwa women wear small ornaments both as a sign of feminity and for enhancing beauty. The names of the traditional ornaments worn by *maargi libinge* (women) on specific occasions are- *lo* (beads), *muri thop* (vermillion dot) *kholing* (ear ornament) *khaila* (ear-rings) *Khaarn* (barles), *yestran* (ring), *kungbali* or *kunkhaoile* (nose ring) and *yathong khaarn. Khosong* (comb) is used to put hair is order. *Aarshi* is the name given is mirror where they can see themselves.They wear silver or bead necklaces and ear-rings. Formerly womenfolk wore ornaments lie *gaamkhaaru* (bracelet), *sipaatmoni* (necklace), *gotaakharu* (bracelet), *senpatia anguthi* (rings) but today these are not much in use. The school going girls wear factory made ear-rings and bracelets which are cheap. Formerly the menfolk used to wear *sihaa* (ear rings) made of gold and silver. Tattooing is however absent among the Tiwas. Tiwa women have long hair while the menfolk keep their hair short.

Shelter

M. Deori writes that *"Charibhai Charikora devata* imparted the knowledge of house construction to the Tiwas and this belief is still prevalent among them."[33] He writes that *"chaamaadi* or *dekaachaang* was the first example of house construction and from it better houses began to be constructed." He gives an account of how the Tiwas got mingled with divine beings and acquired the knowledge of house construction and the circumstances that led to the birth of twelve *kuls* (clans). According to him if any individual Tiwa decides to construct a house, the *nubaar* or *barghar* would be constructed first. This is built in front of the main house in an east-west direction for *deo puja.* Sometimes it is also built in a north-south direction. After selection of the site of the *barghar* the plan for other part of the house construction takes place.

Construction of a new house or renovation is generally done in the months of December/January when local building materials are mature for collection and manpower is available from *dekakhel* and after the agricultural season is over. At present many well to do families in the plains construct their houses with cement and corrugated iron sheets.

In the traditional system the selection of the site of the house or granary is done by the owner or *ojha* (magician) by divination. On the evening of a Wednesday, a handful of rice tightly wrapped in a plantain leaf is put into a hole in the ground at the proposed site and left for the night. If the packet remains intact, the Tiwas believe that the site is favourable. There is another method. The owner keeps a spear on his chest and arms spread sideways and utters incantations. The sign is favourable if the spear remains in its position.

The building materials of a traditional house which comprises of bamboo and *thatch* (long grass) are generally obtained from the jungle nearby.

M. Deori writes that before the bamboo and trees are cut, prayers are offered to *Chaari bhai Chari Kora devata* as he is their creator. For the roof, he writes *soron kher* is required and for procuring it the deity is to be propitiated. It is only after observing *langkhun* and *Khaaplangrawane pujas* that trees, bamboo and thatch can be obtained.[34]

The plains Tiwas generally construct their houses on plinths facing east and south. Thatch is used for the roof, though many who can afford use corrugated iron sheets these days. Walls are made of reeds and bamboo and are mud-plastered with a mixture of clay and cowdung by the *haadaari khel* group if assistance is sought. Generally bamboo posts are used in their houses but the well-to-do use wood. The framework, walls and roof are constructed by *dekaakhel.*

The plinth of the cooking house (*barghar*) is raised about two feet above the ground in order to distinguish it from the other apartments or cottages. The *barghar* has two rooms, one meant for the household deity and the other for cooking purposes. The hearth is considered as sacred and entrance to the place is restricted. Usually, the room towards west is used for the household deity. The main post of a *barghar* called *thunaakhutaa* does not touch the beam and is fixed only after the completion of the construction of the house. Except *gamari* wood no other variety can be used for *thunaakhuta*. If such wood is not available, bamboo may be used. Except *gharbura, zela* and *haari kunwari*, nobody should go near the *Thunaakkuta. Choraaghar* is the outhouse and is constructed a few yards away from the main house where the guests are entertained and the bachelors sleep at night. Now a days the *choraaghar* is replaced by a portico or an additional house near the main house in most Tiwa villages. In between *choraaghar* and *barghar* there is a *maajghar* which is used for sleeping purposes. The *maajghar* has two or three rooms.

The granary is constructed towards the east and certain taboos are observed in connection with the granary. Those who do not possess granaries, a corner of the living room or the *choraaghar* is used for this purpose. The courtyard in front of a homestead is used for drying paddy, threshing and such other activity. A house is encircled by bamboo fencing as stated earlier.

A socio religious ceremony is performed at the time of first occupation of the house in the presence of the *ojha* a of the village and the *borjelaa* of the clan. According to this ceremony the *ojhaa* would remain outside the house while the *borjelaa* would be inside occupying a position in the centre of the *barghar* which separates the kitchen and the dining room. The *borjelaa* would enquire from the *ojhaa* if the house is free from evil influences and if the house could be occupied. If everything is alright the *ojhaa* would answer in the positive. He lights a fire and carries it inside the house and places it in the hearth.

Hill Tiwas

Agriculture

In thc hill villages, paddy is grown both by jhum or shifting cultivation and wet cultivation. In the jhum system, a plot in the jungle is cleared in the dry months before the onset of monsoon. The vegetation is cut and dried and allowed to dry. It is then set on fire and the resultant ash is mixed and hoed thoroughly with the soil so that it is not washed away by the rains. If there is heavy rainfall or even drought like condition the entire crop may be a failure. Wet days are avoided for sowing. Selected paddy seeds only are sown. Several varieties may be sown in the same plot. Generally eight to ten paddy seeds are put in a hole with a pointed stick. The holes are dug by men, while women put in the seeds and cover them with earth.[35]

A mixed cropping pattern is adopted by the shifting cultivation.

Along with paddy, sesamum, cotton, maize *kumura* (gourd), egg plant, chillies, cucumber, sweet potatoes, arum, ginger, turmeric and yam are grown together. The monsoon showers help in sprouting. Paddy ripens and is harvested between August and September. The other crops are cut when they are mature. The main varieties of paddy grown by shifting cultivation are *khaki, para, ashu, changing, birung* and *naga*. As shifting cultivation is of mixed crops, two huts are constructed one is on a high platform of bamboo for keeping watch on wild animals at night. The second is on the ground for watch during the day. The cultivation may take shelter there from sun and rain and at night a small fire is lit near it. The man who guards at night stays in the upper hut. Shifting cultivation is done to supplement availability of food and also to increase purchasing power. Non availability of flat lands for wet paddy cultivation compels the hill Tiwas to turn to shifting cultivation, but they always like to change over to wet paddy cultivation where ever land is available. The first weeding is done soon after the seeds sprout in the month of July. During the first and subsequent weedings constant attention is required, so the women wake up at three a.m. to prepare the morning and mid-day meal which comprise of boiled rice, boiled vegetable, dry fish etc. for the family members who will be working in the fields. After taking the morning meal, they leave, carrying the food packets in baskets called *kho*[36]. The baskets are placed on their backs. A long string of bamboo woven well by the menfolk attaches the basket to the head and this piece of string is called *sedar*[37]. Earlier new plots were used by the slash and burn method. Each Tiwa village these days has a definite area within which it should confine its shifting cultivation. The Karbis who also inhabit those areas do not allow new areas for shifting cultivation. B.K. Gohain writes "Karbis being the dominating tribe with their own people at the helm of affairs in the District Council they do not usually allow the Lalung neighbours to claim new areas for shifting cultivation and in fact most of the Lalung villages have been hemmed in by Karbi villages which have the backing of the District Council where the representation of Lalungs is rather poor". The Tiwas leave a plot of land fallow so that productivity of the soil is retained.

Though they also practice wet cultivation like the plains Tiwas they do not use cow or buffalo to till the soil. Men and women together dig the earth in the fields and fill it up with water and use their feet for making the land suitable for cultivation.

Several varieties of wet paddy are grown, the more common ones are *pathisaaraa, thingrimaai, chingrimaai, jogaamaai, maaikhaaraa, paaraamaai, mikhirmaai, choloukuthimaai*, and *laabramai.*[39] Rice which is produced is their staple food and it is also used for brewing rice beer called *zu*. The normal practice is to transplant seedlings from the seed bed but sometimes seeds are directly put in the irrigated fields. This is generally done in the month of June. But transplanting is done between June and continues upto September. Fields are kept irrigated till the seedlings take root and start growing. The irrigation process is done by diverting water from perennial streams by means of canals or channels dug along natural slopes and cavities. B.K. Gohain points out- "Generally a valley in between hillocks is selected for wet paddy cultivation. A river or a stream originating from the hillock is blocked at the foot hills and the water is diverted to the fields of the valley by canals. Sometimes bamboos are used for carrying the water as ducts to the fields"[40].

When the crop ripens, it is ready for harvesting which generally commences in December. Any villager who is in need of additional hands in agricultural operations may seek help of the *chaamaadi* boys by offering areca nut with betel leaves and rice beer to their leader- the *chaangdoloi.* Acceptance of the same implies help would be rendered. The usual charge is rupees five to ten per day. Every work undertaken is generally completed in a day. They set out early in the morning and work till it gets dark. At noon they take rest and partake food provided by the household for whom they work. The officials do not work but play on flute and drum as well as sing songs to relieve monotony of the others. The boys of the dormitory go to work in the field singing songs and with beating of drums. Singing and beating of drums is an essential activity associated with cultivation like sowing and harvesting of paddy. This is called *deka jowaa*[41]. The beating of drums continues throughout the day to relieve the monotony of work. The stalks are cut six centimeters from the root accompanied by songs and this is called *mai raawaa* by them[42]. It is then kept piled up in the field itself and is well covered with hay to protect it from rain and moisture. These heaps are called *maaiphui*[43]. Separation of paddy from stalks is done in the field itself by beating with sticks by a group of boys and girls. Another method of separation of grains from the stalks is by dancing of young men over the paddy with beating of *khraam* which is called *maipathala*. Unlike the plains Tiwas who store their paddy in the granary the hill Tiwas keep their paddy covered with straws and thatch in *maiphur* (an indigenous circular basket like structure) by tying and covering it up well. They are kept in their homes along the walls in the *nomaji* (outer room) and *nukthi* (room with hearth in it) on raised platforms to avoid moisture of mud floors. While the *maiphurs* are taken home the boys sing all along the way since it is a joyous occasion and this is called *mai missawa* in hills.[44] Whenever it is required for consumption purposes, it is *husked* in the *thinkisaal* by the *thinki* (*dheki* in plains villages) which is a feminine job. The entire process of transplanting, reaping the paddy, separating the grains from the stalks is done paying obeissance to goddess Lakshmi (goddess of wealth). Paddy is sometimes kept in bamboo made containers called (*khosa*). It is covered by a bamboo cover called (*khidri*) in colloquial language. At present, there is a noticeable change in agricultural produce. The Tiwas have started cultivating bamboo, brooms, ginger, turmeric, pears and betel leaves on a commercial scale as a result of which there appears to be an economic change in the hill Tiwa villages.

Besides paddy and vegetables, the hill Tiwa villagers grow a number of citrus fruits which include oranges, *robab tenga* (a sweet sour indigenous fruit), peaches, etc.

The Tiwa Calendar

The twelve months is a Tiwa dialect are *phrndasa* (April 15-May 16), *phokaiphol* (May 15- june 16), *Ordomsal* (June 16-September 15), *laamkhonaa* (September 15- October 15), Khumwali (Oct.16-Nov. 15) *phurdomaisal* (November 16-December 15), *Chumaili* (December 16- January 15), Saalshot (January 16-Feburary 15), Poraso (February 16-March 15) and paashaas (March 16-April15).

The Tiwa calendar is divided into four seasons (*pothor tusi*) namely, *harna pothor* (summer period), *parisa* (the rainy period), *sigaam pothor* (winter), *halor pothor* (spring). The months have native names and they follow the Hindu calendar.

Agricultural Implements

The agricultural implements used by the hill Tiwas are *khangra, paku, khaji, ruwa. Khangra* is a bush knife used for a variety of purposes – like making fine bamboo strips for making baskets as well as for chopping firewood. It is used for chopping off branches of trees, for clearing the bush, etc. *Paku* is the hoe used for digging holes and loosening the soil around the plants. *Khaji* is a dented sickle with a short wooden haft generally used to reap the ears of corn. *Ruwa* is the common axe fitted with a wooden haft. It is used sparingly as majority of work of cleaning the jungles is done by the *khangra*. Only those unmanageable are done by *Ruwa*.[45]

Haadari Khel

In both plains and hill villages, labour if required is organized on reciprocal basis for helping in the agricultural operations and other activities such as in house construction (mud plastering of walls) etc. This system of reciprocal help is called *haadaari khel* system. The men form a *haadaari khel* also called *mewa libing hawe* in the villages. There is no leader in the group. Anybody may join who needs help and has therefore to render help. In a village several groups may be formed. These groups go for works for a specific work only.[46]

There are two *haadaari khels* for females, in the hill villages, one for the girls and the other for the older women. The *haadaari khel* of girls is called *kharlaraw,* while that of older women is called *puri*. There is also the practice of reciprocal help in a small way called *kil* system. In the *kil* system, few may be called such as the neighbours to help in cutting bamboo shoot for example, which is to be preserved. As mentioned earlier, any villager who may require help in agricultural activities may approach the *chaangdoloi* (leader of the youth dormitory) with a pot of traditional beer. Acceptance means help would be rendered and the young boys would work and complete it in a day and would be paid.[47]

Food

In the hills too, rice is the staple food and is taken three times daily. Unlike the plains, hill Tiwa villagers do not take *poita bhaat* (left over rice, soaked in water) as their first meal of the day. If the family members are to go to the field early, the housewife would wake up at three in the morning and cook both the morning meal as well as mid-day meal. The first meal of the day (*phrungimaijawa*) consists of boiled rice (*mai*), boiled vegetables and dry fish. Sometimes *khaar* (alkali) is put into the vegetables and sometimes bamboo shoot (*moiha)*. They take their food with a lot of chillies (*chalu*)[48]. Oil is very rarely used. Instead they fry sesamum and grind it to form powder and sprinkle them over curries and vegetables and sometimes take the sesamum powder separately in the eating plates as an appetiser. If they are in a hurry in the morning, they take only *mai* and *sokrakharee* dry fish prepared with *khaar* and sesamum powder. While going to the fields they take with them *maipantha* (food comprising of rice, vegetables, dry fish etc, wrapped well in banana leaves) as stated earlier in baskets called *kho*. They take pork and chicken very sparingly. They generally eat whatever they produce and what they can collect from the jungles like varieties of edible leaves which include *saag, tenkha, samsuri, famjarilai, lai sadap, thagon,* etc. *Naflang sukuti*, is a famous delicacy among the hill Tiwas. They dry fish and put it in long bamboo containers by grinding it and store them for the year. Another favourite delicacy is *moiha.* From *moiha, tamlong, kurji,* etc are made and stored for the year.[49] Over and above this, the sesamum leaves are dried, powdered and stored and are used when vegetables are scarce. The hill Tiwas call the system of cooking vegetables in this manner as *sagrakhari*. In all there are three ways of cooking vegetables among the hill Tiwas - firstly when vegetables are cooked with *sukuti* it is called *naflangkhari,* secondly vegetables which are cooked with *kala-khar* are called *khaardikhari* and thirdly vegetables which are cooked without *sukuti* and *khar* is called *tankhrekari.* Women coyly admitted of taking rice beer in small quantity to relieve monotony. Menfolk take it more often. They collect water from streams which are perennial. A long bamboo is attached to the mouth of the stream and females and young boys can be seen collecting water in pitchers to their homes.

Household Utensils

Some of the utensils used by hill Tiwas include the following:

(i) chulaw-container to serve rice beer on various occasions-

(ii) chudrar-container to serve rice beer
(iii) khochapa-bamboo container to keep clothes
(iv) mindu-a container where rice is boiled
(v) sagarmindu- a container where vegetable are boiled
(vi) shagoni- strainer for filtering traditional beer.
(vii) sa mindi- container to boil water
(viii) tilao-kettle which contains boiled water ready for drinking purposes.
(ix) thokli- container to carry water, pitcher like item.
(x) khamli- a slightly raised wooden platform used for sitting purposes.
(xi) shada- dustbin
(xii) wasi- broom to clean
(xiii) sharm – a round wooden piece where rice is pounded.

Fishing

In the hills too, the villagers go for fishing in the *Amphi, Umiam* and other rivers. Their method is by poisoning of rivers or streams by smashing wild roots called *pisi* which they put into the river. The poison has the effect of stupefying the fish which float on the surface of the water. They are then caught easily. This system however destroys many immature fish. Another way is by blocking the river and putting a bamboo made trap called *khoka.* This method of blocking of the river and catching fish is called *panasawa* by them. They also use *tingri* to catch fish. Community hunting is no longer done both in the hills and plains, but occasionally wild boars and deers are killed quietly.

Poultry

The hill Tiwas rear both pigs and fowl for sale and for ceremonial occasions. There is a separate shed for pigs built just outside their gates. They do not take eggs but keep them for purposes of divination and for ceremonials. They earn good income from the sale of poultry.

Crafts

The hill Tiwas are skilled in the art of making cane and bamboo objects which they require in their everyday use - *dola, saalani, dhaari*, basket etc. They can also make a *botaa* (traditional plate of stand). They also make the *daaron* which is the traditional rice beer server. They also make their own strings from the barks of trees which are used in storing the paddy in baskets.

Spinning and Weaving

The hill Tiwa women weave their own clothes as well as the clothes of men. They take out thread from cotton which they grow and dye them with various colours and then weave. Almost each and every household possesses a loom which is generally placed in the front side of the house. *Maatisaal* is a way by which the hill Tiwas weave. The hill Tiwa women tie the threads on their waist and weave beautiful designs. They weave *phaskai, kasong, taglaa, taanaa, aanhola, kramsa, nawajil* etc. It is difficult to find a groom for a girl who does not know how to weave. So mothers generally train their daughters in the art of weaving at a tender age. Dyeing is generally done by them with different varieties of leaves and fruits.[52]

Clothing

The hill Tiwas have their own traditional clothes in which they are attired in their daily life. Both men and women wear different coloured clothes which are generally woven by women. The menfolk wear *paguri* which is a piece of cloth wrapped on the head which they call *phaga* or *phagu*. They wear a sleeveless jacket to cover the upper portion of their body and this traditional jacket is called *taagla* in their dialect. To cover the lower portion of the body,[53] a piece of cloth is used which they call *taanaa* or *lengti*. The *lengti* is a narrow strip of cloth about ten hands in length. Some flowery designs are woven with red threads about three inches in breadth on both ends of the *lengti*. Wearing of lengti does not indicate the economic status of the wearer but is the traditional garment of a male Tiwa. On festive occasions they use a piece of cloth draped over the body from the shoulder and this is called *thenus*. Some hill Tiwa men have taken to wearing trousers and shirts.

Some of the hill Tiwa women wear a piece of cloth from breasts to the knee which they called *phaskai* or *methoni*. Some of them wear from the waist below a piece of cloth which they call *kasong* which is equivalent to *mekhela* of the plains Tiwa women. The women who wear *kasong* to cover the lower portion of the body wear a blouse which they call *pharke* to cover the breasts or the upper portion of the body. To tie the *kasong* to the waist they use a waist band called *tongali*. *Juskai* is a piece of cloth worn to cover the entire body from the breasts to the legs. In such cases a blouse is also worn. The garment of an unmarried female slightly differs from that of a married female. Both married men and women wear a band which they call *sawaal* and is a kind of ornament. It is made of old silver coin. The *sawaal* of women is smaller than that of the *sawaal* of men. Hill Tiwa women are traditionally known to wear clothes of bright colours – red, green and black. Some of the educated hill Tiwa girls have started wearing *saalwaar kamiz* like their counterparts in other parts of northern India.[54] The hill Tiwa women wear gold and silver ornaments. The hill Tiwa men wear silver ear-rings and wear copper and brass bangles. On festive occasions both men and women wear ornaments like *saap la, krengla, singli la, mui la* and *khaidong, lothaar, lo'faap, yaastam.*

Shelter

In the hills, a house is built on a rectangular plinth made of earth about 125 centimeters high. Like their counterparts in the plains they too have open spaces in front, back as well as the sides with bamboo fencing all around. In almost all houses, the weaving loom is placed in the front side. The entrance to the compound of the house is by the gate which they call *langra*. The *langra* comprises of a number of short slender bamboo poles placed close to one another and suspended loosely from a horizontal bar on two poles above. One has to push them aside to enter the compound. This creates a lot of noise and thereby alerts the members in the house that someone is entering the compound. Below the *langra* are two wooden pieces attached horizontally to two poles on either side.[55] One has to put a foot inside and the other outside to cross this wooden barrier to enter. Their dwellings are thatched huts, with mud floors. It consists of four parts namely *khomphor, nomaji nukthi* and *thinki sal*. The huts do not have windows and as such it is dark and gloomy inside. The *khomphor* is the front verandah and is used for receiving visitors. The front room is called *nomaji* and is the room where the male members take their meals. As mentioned earlier, baskets of paddy called *maiphur* are placed all along the walls of the *nomaji* on raised platforms. The next room is the *nukthi* and contains the hearth or the fireplace where cooking is done. Beyond the fireplace is a clear space which is used for taking meals and sleeping purposes of the wheres the unmarried women of the household. The last compartment is called *thinkisaal* as the *thinki (dheki)* is placed there. It is used to store the reaped vegetables like gourd, pumpkin etc., besides using it for husking paddy in the *thinki.* Outside the gate a small shed exist for the pigs.[56] There is also a shed where firewood is stored and is called *polphasa* or *polsang*. Raised bamboo platforms are also made outside the gate for drying leaves of different varieties and is called *aam.* The area within the compound is utilized for growing both fruits and vegetables. Vegetables like squashes, papaya, chillies, ground, turmeric, ginger, arum etc and fruits like oranges, pineapples, *robab tenga* (sweet sour fruit) mentioned earlier were seen growing. Earlier there is no specific arrangement for sanitary functions and people used to go outside the house as in other parts of rural India. Of late, pit latrines have been installed in most of households in a corner of the compound.[57] Any visitor to a hill Tiwa village household would be impressed by their clean surroundings. Thus, both hill and plains Tiwas are self sufficient in basic needs and live a very contented life economically.

S.K. Agnihotri points out certain differences in the economy of the hills and plains Tiwas. He states that the Tiwas living both in the hills and plains are almost totally dependent on wet rice cultivation but while the former have developed a system of irrigation necessitated by nature of the terrain, the agriculture in the plains is still largely dependent on the monsoon. Another difference he states is that while cash crops are widely sown in the homestead lands in the plains, the area available for such cultivation in the hills is very limited.[58]

Both the plains and hill Tiwas are labourious by nature and start working hard early in their life and also from early morning. Most of them own land. The soil is also fertile and good climatic conditions prevail in the areas of their habitation. But inspite of this, the crop yield is low. The causes of the low yield may be attributed to old method of cultivation, indigenous tools and implements, use of traditional seeds and manure[59].

Notes and References

1. LA, p.161.
2. *Ibid.*
3. TS, p. 33.
4. *Ibid.*
5. LST, p. 25.
6. *Ibid*, p. 23.
7. *Ibid*, p. 24.
8. *Ibid.*
9. *Ibid.*
10. *Ibid*, p. 26.
11. Sarma, U. et al, *Jagi Bhakatgaon Anchalar Lokasmriti,* Morigaon, 2007 pp. 45-46 (henceforth JBAL).
12. *Ibid*, pp. 45-46.
13. LST, p. 24.
14. LA, p. 49.
15. JBAL, p. 47, alsc see LA, p. 50, Field Study.
16. LA, p.50.
17. JBAL, p.47.
18. *Ibid.*
19. Field Study.
20. Field Study.
21. TS, p. 36.
22. *Ibid*, p. 37.
23. *Ibid*, p. 38.
24. *Ibid*, p. 29.
25. *Ibid*, pp. 39-40.

26. *Ibid.*, p. 40.
27. *Ibid.*, p. 41.
28. *Ibid.*,
29. *Ibid.*, p. 42.
30. *Ibid.*
31. *Ibid.*
32. TS, p. 52.
33. *Ibid*, p. 29.
34. *Ibid*, p. 31.
35. HLG, p. 31.
36. Field Study.
37. Field Study.
38. HLG, p., 33.
39. *Ibid*, p., 35.
40. *Ibid*, p., 36.
41. *Ibid*, p., 28.
42. LST, p., 26.
43. *Ibid*, pp. 26-27.
44. *Ibid*, p. 26.
45. HLG, p. 34.
46. *Ibid*, p. 37.
47. *Ibid*, p. 38.
48. Field Study.
49. Field Study.
50. Field Study.
51. Field Study.
52. Field Study.
53. Field Study.
54. Field Study.

55. Field Study.
56. Field Study.
57. Ali Idris, *'Tiwa (Lalung) Janakristir Ruprekha'*, in Ringchang, 4th issue, 1984, p.425.
58. Field Study.
59. LA, p. 46.

4

Religion

The Tiwas are religious minded and God fearing. They have a very clear conception of God almighty. However, the dearth of written materials on the religion is an area which needs to be explored. Based on empirical study it is evident that amongst the plains Tiwas are the traditionalists or people of indigenous faith who conform to what has been handed down from generation to generation orally and their religion can be described as both theistic and animistic. Then there are others amongst the plains Tiwas who being captivated by the wave of Neo-Vaishnavism/Hinduism propagated by Sankardeva (1449-1568) have undergone proselytisation. Such people gave up their traditional religion, their *kul* (clan) system, *barghar, thaan* worship and thereafter went to *naamghars*. They are called *Saraniyas* as stated earlier. In some plains Tiwa villages of Kamrup there are some Tiwas who have accepted 'Anukul Dharma' but this is a recent development. Amongst the hill Tiwas, there are those who have clung to their traditional religion and there are also some who are Christian converts.

The census reports of 1881 described the *Lalungs* (Tiwas) as using the word *Midai* to denote a God. The western *Lalungs* worshipped a god called *Godal* Margi. The *Lalungs* regarded as sacred the Euphorbia, the madar (*Calotropics gigantea*) and the *gomari* tree (*Gmelina arborea*). This report states – "The manner of their worship is like that of all the wild tribes: a fowl, goat, or pig is sacrificed or on very great occasions, a buffalo, and a simple prayer is put up, imploring the deity to protect themselves, their cattle, rice fields, farm yards and little ones, a banquet of flesh and rice beer concludes the ceremony. The public place of sacrifice is a *thaan* or earthen platform and the *dao* or bill-hook used, on the occasion is a sacred weapon kept on the spot and held worthy in itself to receive adoration. The two great months of public worship are said to be *Phagun* and *Jeth*. Private worship can be performed at any time, as occasion requires...... on the whole, the Lalungs have not preserved their religious notions so well as the Kacharis. Their prayer to Midai is often a curious mixture of Assamese with Lalung words bearing Assamese inflections. The very name of Midai is giving place to Parameshwar or Ram. The deity worshiped in Phagun is known more commonly by the Hindu name of Lakshmi than by Lalung name of Holobuni. Mahadeo and Kali are worshipped in Jeth. In the month of Magh a ceremony called mal, consisting in the planting of tall shaft of bamboo, accompanied by religious rites, is performed on the boundaries of villages. Certain deities called Chari Bhai may be a Hindu rendering of primitive Lalung gods. The names of their priests are also of Hindu origin. The Deoraja fixes the day for the celebration and the Deori kills the victim. Two other officials are the Loro and the Phorongai, the former assists in the celebration, the latter provides the necessary materials. The manner of private propitiation of Midai- by suspending in the house a plantain leaf containing betel nuts and leaves of tulsi and dubari grasses looks like a rite borrowed from the Hindus".[1]

The census of India 1901 described the *Lalungs* as professing animism[2]. This report adds that at the time of Assam Rajas the *Lalungs* are said to have sacrificed eight human victims annually to their gods.[3]

A study on the traditional religion of the plains Tiwas *(Lalungs)* reveal that the *gharburaa, saruburaa, giyaati, deori, zelaa* and *haari kunwari* are the religious personalities without whom religious ceremonies cannot be considered to be complete[4]. The priests entrusted to perform religious ceremonies are called *Loro* in the hills, *Deori* in the foothill areas of *Gobha, Nellie, Khala* and *Sahari* and *Zela* in both the plains and hill areas.

Plains Tiwas

Sanskritisation

That a small section of Tiwa populace chose themselves to convert to Neo-Vaishnavism being attracted to it, gave up their traditional religion and went to *naamghars* and participated in congregational prayers at par with other devotees instead of going to *barghars* and *thaanghars*, giving up their former clan system which tied them together to their society and their adoption of titles of Koch community like Deka, Datta, Rajbongshi, Medhi, Bhagawati, Koch etc., is available in local traditions and the census reports. Such people reported themselves as Hindus and refused to divulge their original tribal identity even in the census reports. The raison d'etre behind their conversion may have been to escape from the expensive and tedious procedures of their traditional religion. It could also be attributed to assimilation and acculturation to the Assamese society the resultant process being called Sanskritisation. The census report of 1921 recorded 3,354 Hindus as against 496 Hindus in 1911[5]. The process of conversion of the Tiwa was similar to that of the Kachari. When he first placed himself under the protection of a Gossain, he was known as a *saraniya*. In this stage he was often free to eat and drink as he pleased, his renunciation of strong liquor and swines flesh must precede his taking rank as a *soru* Koch and when he becomes a *dangor* Koch he was to all religious intents and purposes a Hindu.[6]

The census of India 1901 described the Tiwas as professing animism. The same report further reveals that they also practised human sacrifice. Then there was gradual change over to Hinduism and the census report of 1921 recorded 3354 Hindus and 37,679 animists as against 496 Hindus and 38,723 animists in 1911[7]. By 1931 most of the plains Tiwas in Nowgong reported themselves as Hindus and only 3,500 Tiwas living in the Khasi hills claimed themselves as speakers of Tiwa language and followers of traditional religion.[8] However after the formation of Sadou Asom Tiwa Sanmilan and Lalung Darbar in 1967 a community feeling and a consciousness has dawned and conversion to other religions is on the decline.

Traditional Religion

Gharburaa

The *gharburaa* is the senoir most member and religious head of a *vamsa* or *khutaa*. He is also known as *zela gebi* and *borjelaa*. The selected *gharbura* is inducted to this post after a formal ceremony. The post is hereditary. After the death of a *gharburaa*, his son succeeds him to the office. If there is no son, the post goes to the brother of the *gharburaa*, He is formally accepted by the village elders in the courtyard of the *barghar*. The *gharbura* may be a married person but he must be proficient in the traditional rituals. There are certain restrictions in his diet and movement. *Eeel* and crab are not be taken by him. He may go the cremation ground but cannot play active role in the cremation. There is also the *sarubura* a junior to assist the *gharburaa*[9].

Haari Kunwari

A girl, married or unmarried who assists the *gharburaa* in all socio-religions occasions and in the *barghar* is called *haari kunwari*. She is the youngest female sibling in her generation and *vamsa*. She normally cleans and wipes the floor of the *barghar* and helps in the management of all religious functions of the *barghar*. In the purification ceremony both at birth and death and in all other *pujas*, she plays an important role. A girl from the age of eight or nine years can become a *haari kunwari*. There are certain restrictions in her functioning as *haari kunwari*. She must remain in the family even after marriage which implies that her husband has to be *gobhia* (resident son-in-law). There is no special garment or insignia that for her. Every *vamsa* of both plains and hill Tiwa society has a *haari kunwari*. There is also a *haari kunwari* who helps in socio-religious matters of the Tiwa Rajas but does not stay in the Raja's house.

Giyaati

A male and female *giyaati* (mediator) is selected from amongst the Tiwas to carry out certain religious rites at birth, marriage and death. During death ceremony, the male *giyaati's* responsibility is to perform the last rites in the cremation ground which they call *haathaam* or *hadaam*. The female *giyaati's* responsibility is in the house of the deceased till they reach *haathaam*.

Ancestor Veneration

A great reverence for ancestors and for the deceased is clearly indicated in Tiwas religious ethos (both plains and hills). Ancestor veneration forms an integral part of their religion. In the *barghars*, there are two altars – one for the presiding deity and the other for the ancestors.[10] Appeasement of the deceased with offerings of food, drink and other materials is done at the time of death, During *karam*, food and drinks are offered to the departed soul first by the family members and later on by the others. The Tiwas believe that the ancestors of the household ought to be appeased for they have been elevated to the status of supernatural beings or partners with God, having enough power to aid, assist and bless the human beings on earth. This belief is upheld in the cause of promoting both material and moral well being of the family. This system which still prevails, helps to protect the family from any evil contagion, preserve and observe family taboos and keep intact the ties of kinship. In the month of *Aaghon* (November /December), the Tiwas observe the annual ancestral worship. A meal is prepared for the ancestors and one portion of it is kept at the *barghar* in their name. In the evening it is thrown in an out-of-the way place.[11]

Divination

When human power proves inadequate, divination is resorted to get relief guidance, for ascertaining something auspicious and this has been in vogue among various tribes since the ancient times and it still continues with the Tiwas. Among various rites, breaking of eggs has been most popular and it is still prevalent among them. The signs and omens are read through the yolk. If there are no spots on the yolk, it is a good sign, while spots indicate caution. This tradition has been handed down from generation to generation. The other method of divination is by examining the entrails of fowls. If there are any spots on it, the indication is caution.

Deities

The traditionalists among the plains Tiwas are theistic, but the names of their gods and goddesses differ from clan to clan and from place to place. They do not have image or idol worship. *Fa Mahadeo* identified with god Siva of the Hindu pantheon is their supreme God. He is a benevolent god who showers blessings upon those who worship him with devotion. He is symbolised by the *Zela* or sacred arrow in the places of worship. All worship begins with a prayer to Mahadeo.[12] He is the protector of crops, of fields and of human beings. He is the presiding deity of the *barghar* and of the *chaamaadi* hall in the village. His importance is symbolically demonstrated in the *kheljaawaa* and *chongkong* ceremonies and no Tiwa drinks rice beer without first making an offering to Mahadeo by pouring a few drops on the ground. Kailash is revered as the holy place for the Tiwas as it is the abode of their Lord Mahadeo. At the time of performing any religious ceremony, they pray to God to bring the ancestors to Kailash *Maname*.[13] Another important deity is *Jol-Thol devata* who as his name signifies is the presiding deity of land and water. Other deities include *Bagh Raja, Sani* or *Malthakur, Parameswar, Ganesh, Kuber, Lakhimi, Aai Gosaani, Padumi, Kalika, Kamakhya, Saru Aai, Bor Ai, Aakari, Jagat juri, Kani Andheli*. Another dirty is *Chaari Bhaai Chaari Kora* identified as *Lamkaa Raja*, *Gurubaar*, *Rajeniri* and *Daseniri*. Originally these deities might have signified a group of deities but according to the elderly people that formerly it signified a group of deities but the Tiwas in the present consider the name as that of a single deity.[14] The *Bagh* Raja is considered as lord of the jungle. He is not a benevolent deity but needs to be appeased so that villagers at work in the jungles cutting grass or trees may not be attacked by the tiger. He is given precedence during agricultural ceremonies of *Chongkhong* and *Tusuma* for the fact that agricultural activities cannot be carried out without his permission. There are some *pujaas* which are offered in the jungles by clearing certain specified areas.

Incantations or *Mantras*

Chanting of *mantras* or incantations to appease various dcities and clan gods are recited by the *gharburaa*. These *mantras* or incantations are unwritten but have been handed down orally from one generation to the other and called *bedang*. The *bedangs* differ from clan to clan. The Tiwas do not have any sacred text.

Barghar

The place of worship of each *vamsa* in Tiwa society is called *barghar*. Each household also has a *barghar*. The *barghar* has two altars: one for the presiding deity and the other for the ancestors.[15] Near the altars *Rongdoswari* and *Maidoswari* are placed. In Tiwa dialect *Rongdo* means rice and *maido* means paddy. Every year newly harvested rice grains are kept in a pot near the altar and that is called

Rongdoswori. Similarly, newly harvested paddy is kept in a pot near the altar and that is called *Maaidoswari.*[17] *Pujas* are held in the *barghar* where *gharbura* and *haari kunwari* play major roles. The *Zela* (sacred arrow) and one sacrificial *dao* called *(langkhui)* are placed in the altar meant for the presiding deity. There are customary rules in making and formal installation of the *Zela* in the *barghar*. The villagers of Kamarkuchi who deal in making of iron in implements are generally entrusted with this job. The person who makes the *Zela* has to observe fast. Even while placing order for a *Zela* due honour should be shown to the maker by offering rice powder and betel leaves and nuts. Similar honour should be shown while bringing the *Zela* to the *barghar.*[18]

Thaan worship

Thaans are public worshipping places and may be set up for each village or a group of villages. Sometimes the villages of a particular area may affiliate themselves with *thaans* of different areas. A *thaan* may be described as a large open hall like structure generally set up in an out of the way place near a forest. Public worship is performed in those *thaans* occasionally where the *Deori* presides. Sivaratri and Durga Puja are two important community pujas held at thaans. Other community pujas are Hagara Puja and Basanti Puja. Kalikajaii puja is performed by the Tiwas of certain specific areas. There may be separate *thaans* for different gods and goddesses. Thus *thaans* are found in the names of *Mahadeo*, *Kechaikhati, Bhagawati, Sani, Malthakur* etc.[19] The Tiwas consider the *Mahadeosal* and *Basundhari Thaan* of Sahari Mauza of Nagaon district as sacred. Annual *pujaas* are held in these *thaans* as per direction and guidance of Sahari Raja. Other prominent *thaans* are: the *Mahadeosal thaan, Charibhair Thaan* near Na Khola (Jagiroad) under Gobha mouza, *Burha Gossain Thaan, Uttar Khola Thaan*, *Kesaikhaiti Thaan, Lakhimi Thaan* and *Devi Thaan* in Baropujia Mouza. Some pujas are performed in the forest itself in a secluded area earmarked for the purpose. Whenever a *puja* is to be performed the jungle area is cut and cleared. Such is the custom prevalent in Maanipur village of Morigaon district.

Sacrifices

The main objective of sacrifices is to placate their Gods and prevalent spirits who they believe are responsible in affecting human life in many ways and to bring them to terms so that they do not cause harm. Offering of sacrifices is most essential which indicates influence of Saktism in their religions. The main sacrifices are pigs and fowls, the number of which vary according to the importance of the occasion and in its aftermath cooking its flesh and partaking of it along with rice and rice beer is a common feature. The cock whom they refer to as *ronga rangi chorai* plays a very important role in their religious life. When a *puja* is performed, each household is expected to contribute one chicken along with some rice. Formerly tortoise was also sacrificed before the goddess Kalika, a buffalo or a black goat before Kechaikhati, a duck for Jaleswar, a white fowl for Kuber and a pair of pigeons for Bhagawati. In the Amswoi and Bormarjong area, the hill Tiwas offer black goat to Mahadeo and Maslongar, white goat to Bala Khongor and Botol Maji. In the present day, *maah-prasad* comprising of *mug* (gram) together with different kinds of fruits are offered before the gods and goddesses. The practice of human sacrifice was done away with since 1835. This change indicates influence of Hinduism in their religious life. However, fowls, pigs and goats are sacrificed even in the present. After a sacrifice is performed, the blood is generally smeared on the *bedis* (raised earthen platform) or dropped on different banana leaves (front portion) placed in the ground on the names of different gods and goddesses. Human sacrifice was also resorted to by the Tiwas in the past. This may have been because of their long association with the Jayantias.

Pujaas

Majority of the Tiwas follow their indigenous religion. They perform various *pujas*, both community and individual on various occasions during a year.

Jongkhong Pujaa

In the plains Tiwa villages *Jongkhong pujaa* is also called *Lakhimi pujaa*. It is generally performed after *Bohaag Bihu*. There is another *Lakhimi pujaa* which is observed in the month of *Kaati* i.e. September, October, November. Without observing *Jongkhong Pujaa* nobody should start ploughing. If anybody violates and undertakes ploughing they are fined with a pair of fowl and a pot of rice beer and this fine is utilized in the *pujaa*.

Before the *pujaa* is performed, an area in an agricultural field is cleared by the youths and the *loro, haataari, chaangmaaj, chaangdoloi*, the young and old alike accompany. The *loro* makes a *bedi* (earthen platform) and takes a ritual bath at a pond nearby. On the earthen platform, hundred and ten *toraa paat* (a variety of leaf) are placed, one on top of the other. In front of the *bedi,* seven bamboo sticks are placed in a line. In front of the bamboo sticks, rice beer is kept in a gourdshell. In front of the *toraa paat, aaroi chawal* (a variety of rice grain) is placed. A hen's egg is placed over a silver ring. The *loro* takes sacred water, i.e. water mixed with *tulsi* and *dubari* leaves and sprinkles it over his assistants, the *deori,* etc. to purify them. After that, divination begins. He examines the egg placed on the silver ring and breaks it to see the good and bad signs. If the sign is good it means that the yield of the crop for that year would be good. The *loro* then utters *mantras* to the *devata.* The *jelaa* sacrifices the birds in the name of *devataa* and let the blood drop in the *bedi.* The entrails of the fowls are also examined for good or bad signs. The liver of the birds and flesh from the wing portion is pierced with a bamboo stick while the rest is given for cooking. Those pierced in bamboo are placed in the *bedi.* After partaking in a feast everybody returns home on that day.

After the *bedi* of the *Jongkhong Puja* is made and predictions seen, for seven days, people clean their respective houses as a sign of ritualistic purification. The roads, jungles and outgrowth of the plants are also cleared. Every household makes rice cakes and rice beer. On a fixed day all the villagers go for fishing to a *beel* and the catch is equally distributed. Every household contributes a pot of rice beer, a big *baati* (container) of rice and also firewood. Donations are also collected from the public. The articles given by the guilty who are fined are also put together. On the seventh day, the main *pujaa* or *Jongkhong Pujaa* is performed. The *jelaa* and the villagers go to the cleaned area in the agricultural field on the day of *Jongkhong Pujaa* and discussion takes place whether the *pujaa* would be conducted according to the directions of the assembled villagers or the *jelaa.* The *jelaa* gets busy near the place where *pujaa* would be performed. He would make four *dheeps* (raised earthen platform) one each for *Bagh Raja, Thal devata, Mahadeo* and *Chaaribhai Charikoraa.* On the extreme left is the *bedi* of *Bagh Raja*. In front of this *bedi* a bamboo stick is fastened to the ground and a mango leaf garland is placed along with a gourd full of rice beer. Three layers of banana leaves are placed and over it, is placed *aaroi chaawal* (a variety of rice grains). On top of that a silver ring is placed and on the silver ring a hen egg is placed. The *bedi* next to *Baagh Raja* is that of *Jol Thol Devata*. This *bedi* is divided into seven equal divisions with a knife. At every division is placed a banana leaf (front portion) with *aaroi chawal*, betel nuts and leaves and also *tulsi, dubari* in it. The next *bedi* is that of *Hojaideo Mahadeo*. In this *bedi* a small bamboo platform is made with small bamboo sticks. Beside this *bedi,* a gourdful of rice beer, five pairs of betel nuts and leaves are placed on a banana leaf. To the extreme right is the *bedi* of *Chaaribhai Chaarikara* who is the lord of crops. In this *bedi* two hundred and ten *toraa paat* are placed. On it is placed a silver ring with a hen egg and some rice grains. The priest then performs *the pujaa.* In Maanipur village of Marigaon district tortoise and birds are sacrificed on the occasion of *Jongkhong Pujaa.*

Deo Sewa

Certain mandatory ceremonies are held in the *barghars* each year.[20] It is normally observed in *Kaati* (October-November) or *Aaghon* (November-December) when new areca nuts have ripened and are ready for offering to the deities. In some Tiwa villages, this puja is observed in the month of *Bhaada* (August-September). On the day of the *pujaa*, the *barghar* is cleaned and wiped by the *haari kunwari*. The *gharburaa* removes the old basket (*khang*) made of bamboo which was hung in a corner of the *barghar*. In it were placed the previous year's offerings of nuts, betel leaves, seven packets of rice, seven small bundles of seeds, seven bundles of *dimaru* leaves, bamboo pipes containing water and five bundles of thatch. In its place the *gharbura,* places a newly woven basket with fresh offering of all the aforesaid items. The offering represents the articles of every day use in the life of the Tiwas. The purpose of this ceremony is to implore the deities to ensure that the clan remains self sufficient in basic necessities during the ensuing year. After this *pujaa* the Tiwas start taking fresh betel nuts and leaves.

Kaalikaajaari

Kaalikaa Pujaa is observed in the month of *Kaati* (October-November) to propitiate goddess *Kamakhya* for the well being of the clan and increased yield of the crops. Two tortoises are essential for this *pujaa*. A corner of the *barghar* is selected for the *pujaa*, where an altar is made towards the east. In front of the altar, *'Nibut'* comprising of *moong*, fruits, grams, etc. are placed on a bundle of seven pieces of banana leaves as offering. An earthen lamp is lit in the altar. North of this altar another altar is made where a white fowl and an earthen lamp is placed in the name of *Mahadeo*. The *gharburaa* utters *mantras* and sacrifices the tortoises and the white fowl.[21] A prayer is held and after that the participants partake the *nibut*.

Sani Pujaa

Sani Pujaa is observed in the month of *Jeth* (May/June). This *pujaa* is generally held in an out of the way place. Eggs are essential for this *pujaa* which are sacrificed before the deity. After the prayer, the participants move in westward direction uttering *koi koi* i.e. come, come. When they arrive at the entrance of the village, another *pujaa* is held on the roadside. This is done mainly to scare away the evil spirits.[22]

Hogoraa Pujaa

Hogoraa Pujaa also called *Basanti Pujaa* is observed by the Tiwas living in the foothill areas such as Kathiatoli, Kandoli, Deosal, Maanipur as an annual religious festival. The *pujaa* is observed in the *chaamaadis*.[23] But these days the performance of the *pujaa* is on the wane.

Maal Pujaa

Till a few years back the Tiwas used to perform a *pujaa* known as *Maal Pujaa*. Presently however it is loosing its popularity. Earlier it was observed in the months of *Jeth* (May/June) and *Aahaar* (June/July).[24] The *pujaa* generally started on a Tuesday and four village officials, namely *loro, forongai, koroimaaji* and *gaonbura* were in charge of conducting it. An area was selected for the *pujaa* which was called *maalsasaa.* Two kinds of *maals* are used – *bor maal* and *soru maal. Bor maal* is made of bamboo while stems of small trees are used for *soru maal.* The young boys decorate the upper portion of the *bor maal* with flower designs. The *soru maal* is decorated in the bottom. Four lines about six is to eight centimeters long are made in the bottom of the *maals* which are coloured with turmeric juice or charcoal. Two or three circular designs are carved in the extreme end of the *maals* which are also decorated with black or yellow colours. As soon as the *pujaa* ends the elderly villagers select a few persons to carry the *maals*. Generally, people between forty to fifty years are selected for carrying the *bor maals* while youngsters below thirty are to carry the *soru maals. Bor maal* carriers are to be careful because while they are to beat the roofs of the houses, the flowers on it must not fall down. After that the selected persons proceed to a place where *maals* are placed in rows. They make a *hoi hoi* cry and drummers beat the *khraambar*. The place where the *maals* are kept is called *maal pota*. Small groups are formed and each group carries one pair of *bor maal* and by making *hoi hoi* cry, beat the roofs of the houses. The household then pays due regard to the *maals* by offering eatables and *zu*. In the evening all the groups gather and plant the *maals* below a tree and go back to their respective house. This *pujaa* is observed to relieve the people from epidemics and such other calamities[25].

Bhakat Sewaa

The *Bhakat Sewaa* is held during the month of *Aaghon* (December/January).[26] In this religious ceremony the *gharburaa* and other elders of the clan collectively called *bhakats* pray to God and the ancestors of the clan to bless them with peace and abundance of crops for the year. Early in the morning the *gharburaa* offers prayers to the presiding deities of the *barghar* with betel leaves and nuts. After the *pujaa* the elderly persons of a clan sit in the courtyard of the *barghar* facing western direction. The *gharburaa* of the *barghar* and other members sit in front of them. Betel nut and leaves are placed in *bataas* (traditional plate with stand) and a pot of *zu* before the elderly persons of the clan. A prayer is then offered. At the end, the *bhakats* are entertained with '*zu*'.

Aai Bhagawati

The *Aai Bhagawati pujaa* is observed by the plains Tiwa women in *Pachrajia* areas as the goddess brings peace and progress to the villagers. It is generally observed in the month of *Jeth* (May-June). A raft is made with banana trunk and offerings containing *maah-prasaad* are placed on it. After the prayer, the raft is set afloat downstream towards the west.[27]

The Tiwas also perform some rituals every year for getting rid of evils in the garb of epidemics and pestilence. This is done by the *borjelaa* of each clan assisted by the *ojha* or the village magician.

Rati Sewaa

In some *Tiwa* villages there are *sasang ghar* where the elderly villagers perform the *Rati Sewaa* ceremony. The *Satsang* or *sasang ghar* is a thatched hut with two small compartments and an inter connecting door. No deity is there but only an earthen lamp is lit which is placed on an iron stand called *gachaa*. Though there are no deities, references are made to Purna Sankar Guru, Kalmatri, Tholmatri, Amayaamatri, etc.[28]

There are many individuals associated with the *sasang ghar* with different designations, such as *buraa bhakat*, *saakari*, *saajoni* and *pachani*. The *buraa bhakat* and five or six aged persons form a committee or *parishad* and are in charge of conducting prayers. The *chaakari* cooks rice and the flesh of the sacrificed birds or animals. The *chaajoni* assists the *chaakari* in cooking while the *paachoni* assists all the three office-bearers. These posts are hereditary and do not belong to a particular *vamsa* or *khutaa*.

Raati sewaa is observed either half yearly or annually for the general welfare of the village. But sometimes it may be observed several times on demand by individual households. According to the nature of offerings, *Rati sewaa* may be divided into two – *bor sewaa* and *aaroyaa sewaa*. If pigs and fowls are sacrificed then it is called *bor sewa*, if only a fowl is offered it is known as *aaroyaa sewaa*. Dried rice powder, *saandah*, boiled rice, curries prepared out of banana sprouts (*kalful* or *kaldil*), flesh of pig or foul are offered in *Raati sewaa*. *Bor Sewaa* is generally held in the month of *Jeth* (May/June) while *Aaroiya sewaa* is held in the month of *Kati* (October/November). There are three sections of *Raatisewaa* followers: *Digambaria, Rangasarania* and *Nunmatia*. This ceremony is held in a closed door manner. G.C. Sharma Thakur writes that it is probably done to create a fear psychosis among the common villagers[29].

Individual Household worship

Besides observing certain *pujas* collectively in the *barghars, thaans* and *sasang ghars,* the plains Tiwas also observe certain individual household worship like *Baaro Janiya Bhakat Sewaa, Na Janiya Bhakat Sewaa* and *Saat Janiya Bhakat Sewaa.* For such *sewaas, bhakats* of other clans are invited and they are entertained with feasts. The *bhakat sewaas* are generally observed for the welfare of the family members. The food items have certain specifications. In the *Baaro Janiya bhakat Sewaa,* twelve *bhakats* of different clans are invited, in *na janiyaa bhakat sewa* nine *bhakats* and in *saat janiyaa bhakat sewa,* seven bhakats of different clans are invited.

Individual households observe some other *pujaas* also to appease evil spirits. One such is called *morol pujaa.* This *pujaa* is performed in the courtyard of the household when any family member suffers from a prolonged illness[30]. The courtyard is cleaned well and then circles are made of charcoal powder, turmeric and rice powder. An egg is placed in the centre of the circle. The *deori* chants incantations and breaks the egg in the centre of the circles, the circles are rubbed out and the member of the family who was ill is bathed on the place with magical water.

Religious Beliefs of the Hill Tiwas

Among the hill Tiwas, there are the traditionalists who conform to the oral tradition, that is being handed over from one generation to another. Their religion too is both theistic and animistic like their plains counterparts. Some have converted to Christianity. An analysis of the ritualistic system of the Tiwas, both hills and plains, reveal that their religion acts as a binding force for the group by strengthening shared convictions.

Nubaar

Every *vamsaa* in a hill Tiwa society like the plains Tiwa society has a sacred house which they call *nubaar*. The *nubaar* is the place for offering *pujaas* and prayers to the *Khul devata* and is also used as a living house for its members. This house is constructed in an East-west direction with bamboo, thatch and wood. The first room is called *nomaaji*. At one end of the post of the *nomaaji,* a post called *thunaa* made of *gomaari* wood in the name of the *devata* of that particular clan is placed and it is there that the *borjelaa* of the *vamsaa* offers prayers. It is at the *nubaar* that different *pujaas* of the *vamsa* are performed and discussion regarding the family/families of that particular *vamsa* take place.

Every hill Tiwa family has a *borjelaa* and it is through him that *pujaas* are offered to the lord. In one sense he is their clan guru. He is generally the mother's elder or younger brother. Sometimes any member in the family may also be designated as *borjelaa*. Apart from offering *pujaa* to *khul devata* the *borjelaa* plays a major role in marriages and solving disputes. The resident son-in-law is generally given the responsibility of *borkabir*. Along with the *borjelaa* he also takes an active role in the *pujaas*.

The rituals both at family and group level indicate the prevalence of ancestor worship, divination, theistic beliefs, with a preponderance of sacrifices and 'Zu' libations. A supreme god is propitiated along with other gods and goddesses. Every clan has its own clan gods. There is no image worship. Instead of temples they offer prayers in *thaansaal* and *nubaar*. Pujas are generally performed with sacrifices. Generally, after the *Joon Beel mela* is over, the clan gods are worshipped and kept in satisfaction with sacrifices and other offerings by the *borjelaa* in the *nubaar* for the welfare of the family and to get rid of all unwanted happenings. In the same manner, for the welfare of the villagers and as a precautionary measure from ill happenings, at the directions of the *loro,* the *deoris* perform *pujaas* by offering various sacrifices in the *thaansaal*. It is worth mentioning that the hill Tiwas believe that the various rivers and lakes, hills and mountains have their own gods and if they are not appeased by sacrifices and other *pujaa* offerings, the village will be confronted with untoward happenings.

Ancestor Veneration

Like the plains Tiwas, among the hill Tiwas also ancestor veneration plays an important role in their religious life. The people believe that when a person dies, his soul (*phidri*) goes to God and the dead are elevated to a supernatural status capable of lending material aid to mortals in times of crisis.

Divination

The hill Tiwas like the plains Tiwas believe in divination. They believe that an element of luck is always present in the struggle for existence. As good and ill luck are attributed to superior powers, benevolent and malevolent spirits, the principles of worshipping occult power and of being dependent on divination seems obvious. Almost every ritual is preceded by a divination of which the two most common forms are divination by inspecting the intestines of chicken and breaking of eggs. The liver of pigs and goats that are sacrificed are also used for divination by the *zela* or village magician. After a pig is sacrificed it is divided into three parts[31]. The first portion is for the household, second portion is for the *vamsa* family members and the third portion is for the invited guests. If there is any hole in the liver in the portion allotted to the household, the Tiwas believe that there will be a death in the family.[32] If there are red spots or any cut sign then also it is not considered auspicious but there are ways of relief. If in the third portion, there is any red spot or hole the Tiwas believe that some family member in the *vamsa* or of the public would meet his death soon[33]. In case of sacrifice of goats also, their livers are examined in the same manner.

Deities

The traditionalists among the hill Tiwas worship a number of gods and goddesses but the names differ from clan to clan. In other words each clan has its own clan gods called *khul devata*. For example, the Maslaiwali clan has *Bala Khongor*, *Badalmaji*, *Phurimosor*, *Sonari* etc. The Pumawali clan has *Lang Kheya Khongraja*, *Bala Khongor*, *Badalmaji Singarong* and *Khubilubi* and the *Mangrowali* clan has *Kapla devata*, *Bala Khongor* and *Badalmaji*. The main gods and goddesses of Mithiwali clan are *Silikhongor*,

Lengorbala, Hojaporay, Sonbala, Siliporoy, Phurimosor and *Badolmaji* and those of the *Khoraiwali* clan are *Thalia Thokoria Silkhomai, Polkhomai, Phurimosor* and *Badalmaji.*

There are also place specific deities. In Hamren subdivision in places like Balikunchi, Bor-rongkhoi Gorkhunji, Aasukhunji, Murjipaam, Rongkhoisa and Rongkhoinatral the worshipped gods and goddesses are *Nursing Narab Kamthabroi, Silikongor, Bodol Maji, Sat bhuni* and *Baro-Bhuni*. In Amswai and Marjong areas, *Balakhongor Moramuji* and *Khatbaroi.* In Hadao area *Phorimosor, Amriboroi* and *Bodolmaji*. In Ulukunchi area the worshipped gods and goddesses are *Raipuri, Makundar, Baramahari, Udangkhrong, Horjunbali, Thasmosi, Burha Mahadeo, Mahamaya, Ronsuli* and *Kapla*. The names of other deities are *Sangegiri, Phasegiri, Siliporoy, Hojaporai, Hafoubala, Lengorbala, Thaliya Thokoria, Silkhamai, Polkhomai, Malang, Tohini, Kuru Daini, Uwal Burha, Uwal Burhi, Syakar Burha, Syakar Burhi, Pothor Burha, Pothor Burhi, Khamari, Khumari, Mathine, Kiri, Syang, Kiri, Paguni* etc[34]. Thirty three gods and goddesses mentioned in the Hindu pantheon are also worshipped by the Tiwas in their own unique way and in their dialect. For performance of religious rites and ceremonies, the hills Tiwas have their own *Zelas* (priests) and *Loros*.

Sacrifices

The hill Tiwas like their counterparts in the plains, perform a number of *pujas* with sacrifices. Increase of agricultural yields, protection of crops from insects, and natural calamities like droughts, floods etc. are the oft repeated pleas imploring the deities. Besides that, protection of men, cows and cattle from famine, droughts, epidemics and pestilences are also sought from the various gods and goddesses. To appease the deities and fulfillment of their desires, the hill Tiwas resort to sacrifices. The sacrificed beings could be pigs, goats, ducks, chicken, etc. This shows influence of Saktism. It is learnt from B.K. Gohain that in Amswai and Bormarjong areas the following sacrifices are made for different gods[35].

Mahadeo	:	Black Goat
Pala Konwar	:	White Goat
Botolmaji	:	White Goat

Thalia Thokari	:	Black Goat
Maslongar	:	Black Goat

Pujaas

As stated earlier the hill Tiwas do not have image worship. Instead of temples they offer *pujaas* at *thaansaal*, akin to *thaans* of the plains Tiwas. They offer *pujaa* to Bodolomaaji or Fa Mahadeo and Chaaribhai who are their chief deities. Besides them, pujaa is offered to Balakhongor, Maraamuja, Mohon Fador, Nursing narab, Jokhor buraa, Kabla, Thaaliya Thogoroya and other deities. The *Yaangli* or *Lukhumi pujaa* is performed at the *Yaanglisaal* after every five years in the month of March. During the *pujaa*, goats, ducks, pigeons and fowls are sacrificed but not pigs. There is no specific priest for *Lukhumi thaan* and worship is performed by the *Loro*. The goddess is worshipped by chanting incantations. The young lads (*panthaai*) with *langkhuii* (swords) in their right hands and shields (*Paaru*) in their left hands dance in a circle, the *chaagdoloi* and *chaangmaaji* leading the group.

The *Sogra pujaa* is annually performed in the month of March, after which *Jongkhong pujaa* is performed in *Jongkhong Saal* for sowing seeds. *Langkhun pujaa* is performed in *Laangkhun Saal*.

For the welfare of each village, the *deori* on the direction of *loro* performs various *pujaas* in the *thaansaal*. The hill Tiwas believe that the rivers, hills, mountains, ponds, lakes all have a *devata* (god) and they are to be appeased by *pujaas* and prayers to thwart any undesirable or unfavourable act on the villagers.

During festive occasions like *Sograa*, *Laangkhum*, *Waanswaa*, *Jongkhong*, *Yaangli*, the various gods and goddesses are worshipped. Since agriculture is the backbone of Tiwa economy most of their *pujaas* are associated with agricultural activities and are socio-religious in nature. The village priest or *loro* and his assistant, the *haataari* take the leading role. The office of the *loro* is normally hereditary but if he does not have a son to succeed, the *haataari* may take his place.

Sanikeranne Pujaa Light

The *Jongkhong pujaa* is followed by the *Sanikeranne pujaa* on the following Saturday, which is considered to be the day of *Sani* or

Saturn. The Tiwas believe that *Sani,* the malevolent deity accompanies the other deities during religious occasion's and does not leave the village unless he is appeased and satisfied. The objective behind the performance of *Sanikeranne* is to appease him so that he does not cast his spell or malevolent actions which would harm the villagers. For this *pujaa,* branches of the *modaar* trees are required. Fourteen such sticks cut from this tree are painted alternately in charcoal and turmeric and are used to represent the deity. These sticks called *maalbaris* are placed in a line by the *loro* in front of the *chaamaadi.* After a ritual drinking of rice beer before the *maalbaaris,* all the items necessary for the performance of the *pujaa* like betel nuts, egg, *zu, maalbaaris* are carried to a pre-determined place near the cremation ground. There seven *maalbaaris* are placed resembling a ladder and offering of rice and egg is made in the middle portion of nine concentric circles drawn on the ground. The omens are read by splitting an egg. The purpose of the ladder is to facilitate departure of *sani* from the village to the banyan tree, which is its normal abode. The centre of activity then shifts to the banyan. The *loro* constructs three altars for Mahadeo, Jal Thal devata and Chari Bhai Chari Kora. Certain specific items are placed before each of them. The fowls are sacrificed to appease the deities and while the *loro* carries out other rituals, the flesh of the sacrificed fowls are cooked. The assembled people then partake of the cooked meat. The gathering returns to the village while *Sani* remains on the banyan tree and is believed to visit the village again with other deities when the next religious ceremony is held.

Laijulekhewana Pujaa

After the *Jongkhong pujaa,* the Tiwa villagers generally plough their fields and sow their crops. A ceremony called *laijulekhewana* is then performed imploring the deity to protect the seeds from pests, birds, animals etc.

Tusuma Pujaa

When the seeds sprout and grow another *pujaa* is performed by the Tiwas and this is called *Tusuma.* Akin to the *Jongkhong pujaa,* four altars are made in the name of four major deities and each deity is offered different items. The Bagh raja is given a cock with spots on it, boiled rice, an egg and betel nuts. Jal thal devata is offered uncooked rice and seven betel nuts, Mahadeo is appeased with a cock, a hen, cooked rice, an egg and a pot of rice beer while *Chaari blai Chaarikora* gets seven hens, cooked rice, egg and a pot of beer. The sacrifices are offered according to traditional rituals and bears close semblance to the *Jongkhong pujaa* where *loro*, *haadaari* and *ojha* play their respective roles.

Washirawane Pujaa

While the crops grow and after the *tusuma pujaa* another *pujaa* is performed called *washirawane*. The objective behind the performance of this *pujaa* is to propitiate *Chaari bhai Chaari kora* so that the villagers can go to the jungles and cut the matured bamboos required for either constructing a new house or for renovating the old one. The villagers are free at this time of the year because their crops are growing and maturing and at the same time the bamboo which is essential for all construction activity has also grown and matured. In this *pujaa* an altar is made in the jungle by clearing a certain area in which the *Jongkhong pujaa* is performed. There offering of rice, egg, rice beer and the blood of a cock is made. The egg is split and the chicken or cock is sacrificed and its intestine is examined for reading the omens. A split bamboo is also offered to the deity. After the *pujaa* with traditional rituals are over, all the assembled villagers take rice beer and the young men dance around the altar to the accompaniment of beating of drums and flutes. The merry making continues in the village and the dancers visit the maternal uncles of each member of the group. The uncles and aunts are supposed to entertain the dancers with food and drink and presents of fowls as a tradition. On the day following the *washirawane* ceremony, the villagers begin collecting bamboo from the forests. Like other religious ceremonies this is followed by the *sanikeranne* on the following Saturday.

Laangkhun Pujaa

The *laangkhun pujaa* is performed at the end of (*Kaati maah*) i.e. early December for four days from Monday to Thursday. On the Saturday, prior to the Monday from which the *pujaa* begins the *chaangdoloi, chaangmaji, loro, haataari* and other main officials assemble at the home of the *deori*. The deity is worshipped by pouring wine on the bamboo. Thereafter the bamboo is cut into eighteen pieces. The ceremony ends with a feast, song and dances.

Maisisa Pujaa

When the winter paddy is ripe, this *pujaa* is performed before harvesting of paddy commences by the *loro* in the *nubaar* of his own clan and by the *borjelaa* of each clan. On the pre-fixed day which is generally a Wednesday the *loro* or the *borjelaa,* as the case may be, goes to his *nubaar* with the senior members of his clan and all partake of rice beer in honour of *Mahadeo*. Then the *loro* or the *borjelaa* goes to the paddy field, plucks a few ears of ripe grain and ties them into separate bunches to represent the numbers of original ancesters of his clan. These bunches are carried to the *nubaar* and suspended over the place where the ceremonial meals are taken. The clan members disperse after drinking rice beer. The completion of this ritual is the green signal for harvesting to begin and also for young men to start preparations for the *Sogramissawa*.

Christianity

Just as Neo Vaishnavism or Hinduism had a profound influence on some plains Tiwas leading to social transformation and their acculturation into Assamese society, so has Christianity led to social transformation of the hill Tiwas. Proselytisation of hill Tiwas to Christianity came first through the Khasi Presbyterian missionaries. They preached Christianity to the Tiwas through the medium of Khasi language. Thereafter, the Protestant Evangelists preached Christianity to the Karbis and the hill Tiwas through the medium of Karbi language. The new converts had to accept Karbi dress, Karbi language and Karbi ways of life while accepting the new faith. The first Tiwa converts were some families from *Barmarjong* who came and settled in the new place called Chikdamadkha and soon afterwards another village Umpanai accepted Christian faith.

In the early fifties some families of Amswai village embraced Christianity. In 1951 they were baptized and the Tiwa Catholic community came into existence. In 1953 another Tiwa village, Umphew became Catholic and the foundation of Catholic Church among the hill Tiwas was laid[36]. The Tiwa Catholic community of Amswai was under the care of the Parish priest of Nongpoh. Father Michael Balwan had gone to Nongpoh in 1958 and under him Christianity spread rapidly amongst both the Tiwas and the Khasis. As the Christian converts were on the rise, it was made into a separate unit of the Nongpoh mission. The Amswai Mission centre was built in 1968. This mission set up many schools for the promotion of education of the hill Tiwas.

The Franciscan missionary brothers came to the Amswai mission centre in 1975[37]. They set up a dispensary there. The Franciscan brothers succeeded in converting three Tiwa dominated villages of Umbarmon, Mokhakhuri and Silangkhudi to Christianity. B.K. Gohain writes "The villages of Chikdamakha, a Christian Tiwa village of Karbi-Anglong have hardly any clear idea about the biblical stories."[38] At Amswai, a big church and separate buildings for a school and a boarding house has been set up. The Christian missionaries bring children of Tiwa families for free boarding and education and in the process have succeeded in getting conversions.[39]

Through the institution of the school and the church, the Tiwas are influenced by new thoughts and ideas.[40] The most important of these is the change in their tribal world view. By pouring scorn on traditional beliefs and customs, the missionaries create a sense of inferiority complex among those who refused to become converts. The missionaries took the trouble to go to the interior areas and the impact of Christianity had its sway in almost all aspects of their life. They were engaged in effecting a break with the "*pagan*" practices of the hill Tiwas.[41] They set up schools and are even today imparting education, social work being an essential part of the programmes of proselytisation. This had a tremendous influence on the minds of the people attracting them more towards Christianity.[42] The humanitarian work through the devoted services of the missionary doctors and nurses gave an added charm to the religious teaching and biblical lessons of other missionaries assigned for education and evangelical work.[43]

In Meghalaya, inhabitants of many Tiwas villages, namely, Maoker and Lomlong have accepted Christianity and they identify themselves as Khasis. However, they have not got Scheduled Tribe (Hill) status as yet.[44] The *chaamaadi* which is their traditional institution is not to be seen in the Christian villages. The *Sadou Tiwa Chatra Santha*, Tiwa Cultural Society, Tiwa Mathonlai Tokhra and other similar organizations have tried to create a community consciousness among them.

A noteworthy contribution of these Christian missionaries, in particular, Father Michael Balwan, to the Tiwa community is the script of grammar and a dictionary in Tiwa dialect. He is said to have come to Nongpoh in the year 1958. He was a devout Christian and took all measures for propagation of Christianity. It was due to his efforts that the number of Christian converts grew in number both from Tiwa and Karbi community. The Karbi missionary Jacob Hanse and Sylvester Teron assisted Father Balwan in conversion of Tiwa and Karbi people to Christianity.

The Amswai mission centre had set up several primary level schools in that area and these schools are imparting education to Tiwa children. Father Albano D'Mello was appointed as Parish priest of Amswai in 1977.[46] Father Augustine Edassery is said to have joined later in 1979. At Amswai there is a huge church and they manage a school and a boarding house as well. They have got constructed separate buildings for this purpose. In one building which I visited there was large scale jam, jelly, pickle making which are well preserved in bottles and kept for sale. This is probably to train the local children in the art of fruit preservation.[47]

In conclusion it may be said that credit for progress in this backward area would go to Christian missionaries as they are sincerely trying to educate the children, though in the process they are trying to get large scale conversion of the Tiwas to their religious faith.

NOTES AND REFERENCES

1. HAG, pp. 230-231.
2. Allen, B.C. *Census of India*, 1901, Vol IV, Assam, Part I, Report, Shillong, 1912, p.,58.
3. *Ibid*, p.136.
4. Field Study.
5. Llyod, G.T., Census of India, 1921, Vol. II, Part I, Re-

port Shillong, pp.126-133.

6. Allen, B.C., op. cit, p. 58
7. Lloyd, G.T., op. cit, p. 53
8. Mullan, C.S., op. cit, p.173
9. LA, p. 80.
10. LST, p. 75.
11. *Ibid*, p. 77.
12. LA, p. 76.
13. Field Study.
14. LA, p.77.
15. *Ibid.*
16. *Ibid.*
17. *Ibid.*, pp. 81-82.
18. *Ibid.*, p. 82.
19. *Ibid.*
20. LST, p. 84.
21. *Ibid.*, p. 87
22. *Ibid.*, p. 88.
23. *Ibid.*, p. 89.
24. *Ibid.*, p. 20.
25. *Ibid.*, p. 21.
26. *Ibid.*, p. 85.
27. *Ibid.*, p. 91.
28. *Ibid.*, p. 93.
29. *Ibid.*, p. 96.
30. *Ibid.*
31. TSRG, Part-I, p. 5.
32. Hamilton, F., *An Account of Assam,* DHAS, Guwahati, 1963, p. 89.
33. RRBS, p.107.

34. Srinivas, M.N., *Social Change in Modern India*, Delhi, 2002, p. 6.
35. Gait, E.A., Census of India, 1891, Assam Vol. I, Report, Shillong, 1892, pp. 230-231.
36. Lloyd, G.T., Census of India, 1921, Vol. IV, Assam, Part I, Report, Shillong, p.103.
37. HLG, p. 65.
38. Pator M., 'Tiwaar dhormiya anusthaanot mod, gaahori, kukuraa, koni, saagoli aadir byabahaar', Ringchaang, 5th Issue, p.471.
39. *Ibid.*
40. *Ibid.*
41. Field Study, *Ibid*, p.72.
42. HLG, p. 65.
43. Field Study.
44. Field Study.
45. HLG, p.70.
46. *Ibid.*
47. *Ibid*, p.72.

5

Festivals

Amusement, relaxation and entertainment in the form of songs and dances, constitute another aspect of Tiwa life-both hills and plains. Based on crops, labour and love, the Tiwas celebrate many festivals, at different times of the year. The festivals of the people are closely connected to their religion. The important festivals which they celebrate are *Bisu, Barat, Sogra Missaawaa, Waanswaa, Yaangli, Khelswaa, Laangkhun, Muinaari Kaanthi*, Christmas, Easter, Good Friday, New Years Day, etc. with different programmes which include varieties of songs and dances.

Musical Instruments

The musical instruments of the plains Tiwas are not many. They consist of a few drums and wind instruments made of bamboo. There are several varieties of drums and special uses are assigned to some of them. Among the traditional musical instruments of the plains Tiwas are *khraam, khraambar, tumbang or dogoraa, thuraang, paangsi, dhool, kali, gogona, tokaari*[1]. The *khraam* is a small drum while *khraambaar* is a big one. *Khraam* is longer than *dhool* (drum) and resembles a *khool* (a kind of drum). It is used in almost every occasion, but not the *khraambaar*. The *dogoraa* resembles a pumpkin in shape and two sticks are used to beat it to produce the desired effect. It is a small kettle drum. *Tokaari* is a stringed musical instrument played with the finger, like the guitar. *Thuraang* is a long bamboo flute while *paangsi* is a small one.

The hill Tiwas are also fond of music and songs. Among their musical instruments are various kinds of drums or *khraams*, such as, *khraambaar* (*big drum*), *khraam panthai* (small drum), *tumding tagar* (put around the waist and played like a tabla, a kind of drum), *thakaari* or *tokaari* (a stringed musical instrument played with the finger, like the guitar) *saaraangkaat* (violin), *komona* (wind instrument made of bamboo) and among the flutes are *paangsi, thurang* (long flute) and *muhuri* (*a horn*) are used.[2]

Songs and dances are performed not only on important religious occasions, but also on various other occasions, such as, *mindai khrona* (prayer song), *chaamaadi loa* (construction of *chaamaadi*), *khrom nanga* (community ploughing), *mai rawa* (harvesting of paddy, *mai pathala* (community threshing), *mai missawa* (bringing paddy bundles to the granary, *waanswaa* (grinding of rice), *khel jaawaa, aahoi luwaa* (welcoming the goddess of wealth), *faang sokaa* (cutting trees), *pan thai pioa* (returning of youth from forest, paddy feids), *dakhra pala* (dancing with two long pieces of bamboos), *tomere kowaa* (circle dance), *rongkhon* (*dhanesh* bird dance), *pere* (crab dance), *mothal* (squirrel dance), *pira nritya* (dance with a wooden stool with very low stands); *haakhel* (plough dance), *kathor kasowa* (preparing the land for transplantation of paddy), *laangkhun* dance during cutting of bamboos[3]........

Lo Ho La Hai and *Lali Hillali* are two songs sung frequently on different socio religious functions. G.C. Sharma Thakur gives a few specimens of :

Lo Ho La Hai song as

'Lo Ho Laa Haai, Lo Ho Laa Haai

Lo Laa Heloyaa Laai

Bhaai Oi, Laa Laa Heloya Laai

The leader *(Ojhaa)* leads the song while the *paalis* (assistants) repeats the same after him

'Ojhaa'	:	*'Kino Mas Mariba. Sole Mor Bopai Oi,*
		Kino maas Maaribaa Sol, Bhai Oi
		Laa Laa Heloyaa Laai
Paali	:	*'Lo Ho Laa Haai*
		Lo Ho Laa Haai
'Ojha'	:	*Abujan Bhaiyeke Bujabo Nuware*

Dhonde di Saraki Gol
Bhai Oi, La La Heloyaạ Lai
Pali : *Lo Ho Laa Haai*
Lo Ho Laa Haai

'Lo ho means rhythm or tune *laa* means slowly and *Haai* means loudly, *Holoya* means, carefree and *laai* means proceeding while dancing.[4]

Another important song of the Tiwas is *Laali Hillaali. Laali* means a line having no end and Hillali means waves or variation of tones. Thus, *Lali Hillali* means series of songs having no end like *waves* of sea which come one after another ceaselessly. Generally these songs are sung between two person's male and female in question answer type series. While singing these songs the leader and his followers are served with rice beer and unless sufficient quantity is taken, *'Lali Hillali and Lo Ho La Hai* songs cannot be performed in the true spirit.[5]

Bichu Festival

Like the Assamese community the Tiwas living in Assam also celebrate three *Bihus-Bohaag Bihu*, *Maagh Bihu* and *Kaati Bihu*. with great zeal and enthusiasm. They however have their own way of celebration. They call *Bihu* as *Bichu* and in some areas even as *Pichu*.[6]

Bichu is a festival centering around agriculture. As stated earlier like the Assamese people, the Tiwas also celebrate three Bihus –which they call *Boisaak Bichu, Maakh Bichu* and *Kaati Bichu. Boisaak Bichu* is celebrated in April-May after the agricultural operations are over and people find time for merriment and enjoyment. Nature herself bestows a new festive atmosphere at this time of the year with new foliage and flowers and the melodious tunes of the cuckoo bird further adds new zeal and enthusiasm. Human emotions too at this time cannot be subdued any longer and people give vent to their expressions in the form of dancing. The *Kaati Bichu* is observed in October-November in a very austere manner as stocks of paddy are depleted. The *Maakh Bichu* is celebrated between January fifteenth to February sixteenth as harvesting festival. The matured golden paddy has already been harvested and there is plentiful to eat.

Bichu days

M. Deori writes, the Tiwas celebrate *Bichu* on Tuesday and Wednesday, but in Gobha, Nellie and Sahari, *Bichu* is celebrated on Saturday and Sunday. Recently the Tiwas have started celebrating *Bichu* on *Sankranti* and this custom continues. However, the Tiwas still consider Wednesday as their sacred day and anything auspicious is generally begun on that day[7].

Khaati Bichu

Like the Assamese, *Khaati Bichu (Kaati Bihu)* is observed by the Tiwas on *Sankranti* day last of the month of *Aahin* (September/ October)[8]. In the morning the villagers go to the paddy fields and plant the front portion of a bamboo in the midst of their paddy fields. The outer covering of *robab tenga* (an indigenous sweet sour fruit with acid content) are spread in the fields. In the evening earthen lamps are placed in the paddy fields. In some villages agricultural implements like *juwali, nangal,* etc. are all taken to the *barghar* and a fowl is sacrificed in the name of *Bihukormi* (*Biswakarma*) who is architect or artificer of the gods to invoke blessings from the Almighty for keeping the implements in good condition. In the evening '*Nibot*' (*noibedya*) is offered and the cattleshed, kitchen, granary and the weaving areas are kept lighted with earthen lamps.

In *Khati Bichu,* in certain areas, at the *barghar* and at *thaans* the worshipped deities are offered newly grown betel nuts.[9] In some other areas in the month of *Bhaada* (August/September) new betel nuts are offered to the worshipped deities in the *barghar* and to the ancestors. This is called *Deosewa.* Unless this is done new betel nuts cannot be used by the *jelaa, haari kunwari, deori,* Raja and other office bearers. Since this *Bichu* falls in the lean period in the agricultural cycle, the celebrations are marked by austerity in comparison to the other *Bichus*.

Maakh Bichu

The *Maakh Bichu* also called *Tomaachi* is celebrated by the Tiwas in the month of *Magh* (January/February) with traditional gaiety. They celebrate *Maakh Bichu* on Tuesday and Wednesday following the *Maakh Bihu Sankranti. Bihu* eve falls on Tuesday while Wednesday is celebrated as *Bihu*. A week prior to celebration of *Maakh Bichu*, the Tiwa villagers are agog with the sound of *dheki* (long wooden structure with a pestle) grinding rice grains into fine powder to make rice cakes called *pithaas*. The manner of celebration is similar to the Assamese with minor differences. Construction of *meji* (heap of firewood) and *bhelaaghor* (improvised shed of paddy stalks or dry banana leaves) is completed two or three weeks ahead. Generally teenaged cowboys called *gorokhias* construct these structures with great zeal and enthusiasm. These *gorokhias* select a leader amongst them and he is called *borgorokhia* and every *gorokhia* is supposed to carry out his orders. Among the hill Tiwas the person who in a charge of *meji* and *bhelaaghar* construction is called *mohaal*.[10] In some areas, the Tiwas construct separate high *mejis* for *Raja*, *Kuwari* and *Senapati*. In the present day in the plains areas there is no custom of constructing a high *meji* in the name of the Raja and the *Senapati*. But in the foothill areas of Gobha, Nellie, Khola and Sahari such a system still exists.

On the eve of *Bichu*, the revellers, youngsters of the village spend the night at *bhelaaghar* by lighting bonfire, singing and dancing. At dawn they go to the Raja, *Senapati* and other officials' house to fetch them. The Raja and *Senapati* take bath with turmeric and gram paste and when the *meji* is lit in their honour they take the warmth from it. For the convenience of taking bath, the *mejis* are generally constructed on the banks of *pukhuri* (pond), *beel* (lake) or *noi* (river). After the *Meji* has been fully burnt the Raja and his officials retire to the *Paatchoura*. The *paatchoura* is the place where the Raja wears and changes clothes. Here itself the Raja is shown respect and honour by the Tiwa villagers by prostrating before him and then they return home. In the Khasi hills, Tiwas do not follow the custom of constructing *mejis*.

In some areas, particularly Baropujia wooden *meji* is burnt at night. They sing and dance melodious *Bichu* songs with beating of the *pisukhraam* (*Bichu* drum), *taal* (cymbal) and *pepa* (wind instrument) made of buffalo horn. *Kaahi naas* (dancing with two bell metal plates) was formerly arranged on this occasion but now a days it is not performed. In Baropujiya however this dance still continues.[11] In some villages while arranging the *meji*, bundles of paddy stalks are placed upside down or in reverse manner and when this *meji* is lit the elderly Tiwa villagers assemble and explain their mistakes regarding *Bichu* organisation and ask for forgiveness.[12] They then partake *Zu*. Till a few years back *Bichu haat* (market) was set up on the day of the *Bichu* where drummers, pipers and singers of *Bichu* songs had to compete with one another in an open field.

In this *Bichu,* the Tiwas worship their deity in the *barghar* with offerings of *sandoh* (fried rice grains which is pounded) *pithaas* (rice cakes) *Zu* and other food items. Special offerings are made to the ancestors also. In some villages offerings are made at *Sasanghaar*. During the day the villagers, unlike other days do not take cooked rice. In the evening the youngsters prostrate before the elders and then take food. But before partaking of food, rice and *zu* are first offered to the ancestors in the front portion of a banana leaf. In the kitchen, granary, cowshed and the weaving place, earthen lamps are lit in the evening.

Joon Beel Haat

One of the most attractive features of the *Maakh Bichu* celebration is the holding of a *haat* (market) annually near Jagiroad renowned as *Joon Beel Haat* (market). According to some Tiwas, the market (*haat*) earned its name as it was held on the banks of a *beel* (lake) whose shape resembled a crescent moon. There are diverse opinions regarding the origin of the name *Joon Beel*. Whatever be it the *haat* begins on a Thursday and ends on Saturday generally from seventeenth January or a little later. The *Maakh Bichu* in Gobha area is celebrated on Saturday and Sunday of the second or third week in the month of *Magh*. The *haat* is the venue of conglomeration of both tribal and non-tribal people of both hills and plains. The hill tribes belonging to Tiwas, Karbis and others bring home grown products such as ginger, seasame, turmeric, arum, potatoes, lac, chillies, cotton, brinjal, cane and bamboo products and exchange them with dry and raw fish, *sandah* and rice cake of the plains Tiwas. This is a unique feature because barter system of yesteryears which has become almost obsolete is in operation even at present amongst the Tiwas though this is restricted to this *mela* (fair). The Tiwas are thus continuing this tradition. They also bring with them a special packet which is a tax as well as a gift for the Gobha Raja.

Nowaan Jhaawaa

On the day preceding the *haat*, community fishing is undertaken in the *Joon Beel* or near about. The people engaged in fishing give a part of their catch to the Raja as gift and this tradition continues even to this day. The Gobha Raja and his officials sit together on the banks of the *beel* and enjoy a feast together with the freshly harvested rice. Formerly there was a custom that the Gobha Raja would take *sol* variety of fish and rice on the banks of the *beel*. This is called *nowaan jhaawaa*.[13]

Bichu Pujaas

Performing pujaas in the *thaans* are mandatory prior to celebrating *Boisaak Bichu*. If the *pujaas* cannot by chance be performed in time, *Boisaak Bichu* celebration may be deferred to the month of *Aahaar* (June-July). Again there is a tradition that if the Raja did not get to eat *Sol* fish prepared with bamboo shoot, there would not be *Bichu* celebration. The *pujaas* begin from the first week of the month of the *Cho't, Chaitra* (March-April). In the areas which were once upon ruled by the *Saato Rajas* and the *Paacho Rajas* there is a tradition to offer *pujaas* at various *thaans* to the gods and goddesses. In Baropujia, there was a custom of observing *Jongkhong pujaa* prior to *Boisak Bichu* celebration. In *Gobha, Nellie, Khola* and *Sahari* areas also *pujaas* are performed at various *thaans* by their respective Rajas and this tradition still continues. In Nellie area, the deities worshipped on this occasion are *Bardeo* or *Mahadeo*, *Mahaamaai* (*Parvati*), *Jongkhong, Bhagabati, Kalikha, Kesaikhati, Ronsali* or *Ronsondi*. In Khola area the worshipped deities during this festive season are *Burharaamsaa* (Mahadev), *Bhaagabati*, *Kalikha*, *Ronsali* or *Ronsondi*, *Chaaribhai*, *Kesai-Khati*, *Phorimosor* (*Surya devata*). In Gobha area *Mahadeo*, *Saribhai*, *Bhagabati*, *Kesai-Khati*, *Swapnamajika* (weather god), *Kalika* and in Sahari area *Mahadeo*, *Basundhari*, *Ganesh*, *Kartik*, *Bhagabati*, *Ronsali* or *Bauli Khunguri (Kunwari)* and other gods and goddesses are worshipped. Each of these gods have their own separate *thaans*. There are some *pujaas* which are not held annually but every five years, for e.g. *Phorimosor Pujaa*. In each of these *pujaas* the gods and goddesses are offered with newly grown fruits and only after such offering, the Rajas and their officials partake them. In Khola area, only after all the *pujaas* are over, the Raja and the *Senapati* offer individual *pujaa* to *Hojaideo* or *Mahadeo*. In Sahari area, on the *Bichu* day itself *Ganesh* and *Kartik pujaas* are performed. The Raja himself puts a silver flower on the stone-carving of *Basundhari* at *Basundhari thaan*. Prior to this at another *Mahadeo thaan* near Jongal Balahu's fort, the Raja offers a silver flower.

Boisaak Bichu

On the eve of *Boisaak Bichu* all the fruit bearing trees are tied with paddy stalks. In some areas this is done on the *Bichu* day itself. It is believed that such action increases productivity or the fruit bearing capacity of the trees. On *Boisak Bisu* eve or on the day of *Bichu* itself *bhaang* and *posotia* (varieties of leaves) are cultivated in newly sown paddy fields. On the day of *Bichu*, earth or mud is added to bamboo trees as an offering to the plant as the plant is used for multifarious purposes.

On the day of the Bihu, early in the morning all the villagers assemble in their respective *barghars* and cut vegetables like gourd, brinjal, pumpkin, cucumber, potatoes into small pieces and stitch them up together with thin bamboo strips. The *gharburaa* arranges a *pujaa* in the *barghar* or in the "*khola*" that is, space in front of the *barghar* and a fowl is sacrificed. Formerly unless this sacrifice was made the villagers could not take out their cattle for bathing. However, this sacrifice is not performed these days.

Pujaa is offered to *Chaaribhai Charikora* for a rich harvest, well being of the family members including the domestic animals and safety of precious belongings for the year. In some villages *Bagh Raja* is worshipped for protection of their cattle so that they may not be devoured while eating grass in the fields. 'Kuber' is worshipped in the enclosed area of a household for increase in wealth.

In all these pujas sacrifice of fowl is a must.[14] Lord Mahadeo has to be given a fowl apart from *gram* and '*boot*'. From the manner of death of the sacrificed birds the elderly villagers can foretell the future of the village in the forthcoming year. If the sacrificed bird dies keeping its face towards the earth, the year ahead would be good. If the sacrificed bird dies facing the sky then dry weather would prevail and chances of drought is imminent. If the bird dies facing south-westwards, cultivation would be delayed. During the *pujaa* a mixture of rice powder and water is sprinkled in the granary, cowshed, cooking place and in looms. After the *pujaa* another mixture of ash and mustard oil is prepared and with gourd pieces imprints are marked on the bodies of the cattle along with gram and turmeric paste. As soon as they hear the sound of the *pepaa* they take it as a signal to lead the cows to a river or a *beel* for ritual bathing. The pieces of vegetables cut and stitched earlier are fed to the cattle blessing them with good health and productivity.

After the traditional rituals are over a javelin (*jaathi*) throw competition is organised among the villagers for entertainment. A *taamular dhakua* (betel nut cover) is placed at a considerable distance and the aim of a participant or *jaathi* thrower should be the *dhakua*. In areas of Nellie, Khola, Gobha and Sahari a small banana tree is taken instead of *taamular dhakua*. The competition is held clan wise. The participant who could throw the *jaathi* nearest to the *taamulor dhakua* or banana tree is declared the winner of the game. After the end of the game, in some areas, the Tiwas assemble at the *barghar* where they partake arum leaves with chicken or dried fish with a lot of chillies along with '*Zu*'. In other villages people assemble in the *barghar* at mid-day and the *Zela* and the *haari kunwari* offer pounded fried rice, rice cakes and rice beer to the gods and ancestors in the *barghar* with a prayer for their wellbeing. Even in *sasang ghar* in certain areas fried powdered rice, rice cakes and rice beer are offered. In the evening before the cows enter the cowshed, a small fire of paddy husk is lit at the entrance (*poduli*) of each household's compound. When the cows arrive, the fire is fanned and this is done to ward off evil spirits, insect and mosquitoes which may bite them. Water is taken from the *ghoti* or *lata* (pitcher like container) and sprinkled on the legs of the cows. In the cowshed the old *pogha* (rope tried around the necks of cows) are taken out and new ones are tied. The cattle are fed with rice cakes and *sandoh*. All the implements used for agriculture are collected outside the *barghar* and are purified with a mixture of rice powder and water. The next day, Assamese towel known as "*Bihuwaan*" are offered to the elderly persons as a mark of respect and honour. The womenfolk prepare a special curry of fowl and arum leaves. Leaves of *pasatia, koilati, porolati, tulsi, bihlangani, mongamari* are also used in the curry. Besides this special curry, they take an indigenous medicine prepared out of immature jackfruits, *nilukath* and other herbs. The Tiwas believe that taking this medicine would keep serpents away. From this day merry making and dancing begins in the open field for a few days.

Jhuraa Tulaa

Every year in this *Bichu* the *Raj Kunwari* changes the old *jhuraa* and replaces it by a new one in the *barghar.*[15] *Jhuraa* is a packet which contains *aaroi* rice grains and basil leaves wrapped in 'kou' or banana leaves with *dubari* grass. After tying the *Jhuraa* in the *barghar*, the old *jhuraa* is taken out in the Raja's house. This ceremony symbolises welcoming of new agricultural year. *Jhuraa* being a symbol of crop.

Bheti Korhaa

Among the Tiwas of Gobha, Nellie, Khola and Sahari, during *Boisaak Bichu* another ceremony is celebrated called *'Bheti Karhaa'* or 'Rajaar Bhetibhaar'. On that particular day the villagers come from various parts and bring with them shoulder loads *(bhaar)* of locally produced items such as rice cakes, cotton, turmeric, brinjal, chillies, lac, raw and dried fish, bamboo shoots, etc as presents (*bheti*) for the Raja. These items are distributed amongst the Raja, princes, *senapati* and the ladies who sing devotional songs. Along with the main '*bhaar*' small *bhaars* or *chaangi* with tiny pieces of the aforesaid items are also brought. Pieces of small banana shoots are also included. All these are collected in the *chowra* of Raja. Two groups of young boys then engage in a mock fight with these *bhaars*. Each group tries to grab the *changis*. When they manage to snatch the *changi* and pieces of banana shoots they throw them over the *patchouraa* and every time they get it they sing in a chorus:

> *"Tawe phara pisu liu*
>
> *Pisu liu ohiu"*

Meaning from today there is *Bichu. Bichu* goes on. This continues till the *bheti bhaar* snatching is over. In the evening a feast is arranged with the articles of these *bhaars.*[16]

Buka Naach

The hill Tiwas celebrate *Bichu* festival by *buka naach* which is a dance over mud performed by the youngsters of the village and this marks the concluding part of the festival. On the following day of the *Bichu,* the youths of a village gather in a place and seek formal permission from the village elders to perform the 'bukaa naach'. Necessary preparations are completed before noon. The drummers and pipers are formally invited. The young girls and boys dance from house to house starting from one end of the village. The families welcome them in the courtyard with betel leaves and nuts and a few rupees. Singing and dancing continues for seven days starting from Wednesday to Tuesday. On Wednesday to culminate the occasion, some young boys go out in search of a pig. In the meantime, the girls make arrangements for a feast. They all assemble near a *beel.* An ankle deep muddy place is made and near this place the elderly villagers offer a short prayer. The young boys and girls sing and dance over this muddy area for about an hour or so. After that they clean themselves in fresh water and return to the place. Again a prayer is offered. The pig is formally sacrificed and everyone present enjoys the feast together. With this the festival comes to an end.

Gossain Uluwa Utsav

Among the plains Tiwas the *Gossain Uluwa Utsav* or *Melaa* is an important part of *Boisaak Bichu* festival. On the *Bichu* day the elderly villagers decide the date of the festival and necessary arrangements are made. The image or idol of either Vishnu, Mahadeo or Ganesh and sometimes the Bhagavat Gita is placed on a wooden structure and taken out from the *naamghar* to an open field with certain formalities and after singing *naam-kirtan* before the image, it is brought back and kept in its place in the evening.

Regarding the origin of *melaa* or *Gossain Uluw Utsav* there are several legends. According to one such legend, after the acceptance of Neo-Vaishnavisim by the Ahom king Jayadhyaj Singh, the then *Paacho Raja* and *Sato Raajas* of the Tiwas too accepted Neo-Vaishnavism and *melaas* started.[17] As a sign of accepting Neo-Vaishnavism, the Raja and his officials with *dhaal* and *toruwaal* (sword) in their hands would go in a procession while one of them would take the holy wooden structure with an idol in it on the shoulders from the *naamghar* to an open field accompanied by women singing devotional songs. It was in this *melaa* that the *Paacho Rajas* and *Saato rajas* paid their taxes to the Ahom king. Along with the religious aspect, payment of taxes also formed an important part of the *melas*.[18] This *melaa* was held every year and still continues in the month of *Bohaag* and people belonging to various communities conglomerated and enjoyed themselves at these *melaas*.

According to another legend, during the reign of Jayadhvaj Singh, Damodar Atoi set up a new *satra* at North Lakhimpur's 'Basudev *Thaan'* and this *satra* later on become renowned as *Naruwaa* Satra. At the time when Damodar Atoi preached Neo-Vaishanavism at North Lakhimpur he met Chaturbhuj Thakur's *gurus* and along with them proceeded to Borduwa. On their way one of the *Paacho Rajas* namely Mikir Raja Setuwa was given *saran* and Thakur Atoi directed him to hold *doul utsav*. It so happened that the very next year Thakur Atoi had gone to the Mikir Raja's house and learnt that the latter did not hold *doul utsav* as directed and hence expressed his displeasure before the Raja. At this, the Mikir Raja took the holy wooden structure on his head and went for a *padayatra* in his area- Mikirgaon. From that time onwards, instead of holding *doul utsav,* the Mikir Raja would take out the holy wooden structure from the *naamghar* to an open field every year in the month of *Bohaag* and since then *Gossain Uluwa utsav* or *melaa* started.[19]

Lakshisingha Deka in his book '*Monikonwar or Akhyaan*' gives a different view regarding the origin of *Gossain uluwa utsav* or *melaas*. He writes that the Koch king Maharaj Naranayan sought help from the *Saato Rajas*, the *Paacho Rajas* and other Rajas for invasion of Gaur as his brother Sila Rai was held captive by Sulaiman Kararani. In response to his appeal the *Saato Rajas, Paacho Rajas* as well as Rajas of Dumura, (Dimoria), Gobha, Nellie, Khola collected their soldiers and proceeded to Nagaon. Maharaj Naranarayan impressed by the preparations awarded gifts to the soldiers. While the preparations were going on news came of the release of Chila Rai. Later on to commemorate the harmony and unity displayed by the soldiers, Maharaj Mahamaya presented a *Satula Murti* (an idol) and every year on the fourth day of *Bohaag* (April 15-May 16) *melaa utsav* is held this is the origin of *melaas*.[20]

Lokeshwar Gogoi writes that there are two opinions regarding the origin of *melaas*.[21] One group opines that the Mikir (Karbis) and Lalungs (Tiwas) used to celebrate *Chat Bihu* in the month of *Cho't* (March-April). In this Bihu the new soldiers were imparted training in the art of warfare with *toruwaal* (sword) and *dhaal* (shield) in an open field by the Ahom officials. The successful soldiers were rewarded and this award giving ceremony was done during the *melaas*. The Ahom royal officials were also invited to this function. At the same time for the welfare of all, an idol was taken out from its assigned place to an open field and thus *melaas* began. There is also a saying 'Paacho Rajaar Maah Saol, Rahial Baruar Bar Sobha'. The meaning is that the Rahial Barua used to collect taxes from the *Paacho Rajas* which included *saal* fish seeds, bamboo shoots, *khoricha* (made from bamboo shoots) and these were collected in the month of *Boisaak* (April-May).

Another group of scholars point out that to attract the masses, the neo-Vaishnavites started the *Gossain Uluwa melaa*. Sankardev's followers and his grand-daughter Ai Kanaklata preached Neo-Vaishnavism in the north western part of Nagaon. But though the Mikir Raja and Tiwa Rajas embraced Neo-Vaishanivism Saktisim continued among the masses. To attract the masses therefore *Gossain Uluwa melaa* started.[22]

Melaas or *Gossain Uluwa utsav* (festival) is popular in Nagaon and Morigaon areas. It is mainly held in former *Paacho Rajya* and *Saato Rajya* areas and in the eastern part of Kamrup distirct i.e. in Dimoria. Besides these places, *Gossain Uluwa mela* is also held in Gobha, Nellie, Khola Sahari, Bardua, Domal, Mayong. There was a custom of holding *melaas* once a year beginning from the month of *Bohaag* (April-May) till a part of *Jeth* (May-June). *Melaas* are also held in the areas where the descendants of the former Rajas have gone and settled. People belonging to various communities like Tiwas, Karbis, Koch, Kaibortas take an active interest in these *melaas*. In the former Saato Rajya areas, i.e. in Tetelia and Kachari Gaon, such *melaas* are not held. In the past, the Tetelia Raja used to hold Barat *Pujaa* instead of *melaas*. In the Paacho Rajya areas, the Topakuchi Raja first holds *melaas* called 'Burha Melaa'. After Topakuchi, Baropujia,

Mikirgaon, Kakmari, Phulguri, Sorah and Khaigor holds *melaas*. If by chance the Topakuchi Melaas are not held in time, the *melaas* in other former *Paacho-Rajyas* areas also get deferred. The Dandua *melaa* in Morigaon district which is held on the fourteenth day of the month of *Jeth* (May-June) in one of the biggest *melaas*. If *melaa* is to be held at Baropujia then the Raja had to observe *Jongkhong* puja in the month of *Cho't, Chaitra,* (March-April) as a tradition. If this *pujaa* is not observed, then Bohaag Bihu and *melaas* cannot be held because the lord of the crops is *Jongkhong devata* and if he is appeased then the crops will yield a good harvest in the New Year. The Tuesday which falls after the Assamese Bohag Bihu celebration is the day when Baropujia Raja holds *melaas*.

Formerly under every Raja, (of vassal states) one *melaa* was held but that tradition dwindled away and different areas hold *melaas* according to their convenience.[23] Various idols are placed inside the wooden structures. Sometimes, the *Bhagawat Gita* is placed, sometimes the idol of Mahadeo and sometimes, of Vishnu. In Baropujia Raja's *melaas*, Mahadeo is placed inside the wooden structure while the Khola Raja puts the idol of Vishnu along with Ganesh.[24] With the spread of Neo-Vaishnavism. *Bhagawat Gita* is placed in some wooden structures. From this it can be inferred that both Neo-Vaishnavism and Saktism prevails among the Tiwas.

On the stipulated date of *Gossain Uluwa Mela, naam-kirton* is held inside the *naamghar* while *khraambar* is played outside. The young boys carry shields and swords in their hands and dance along with the rhythmical tunes of *khraambar*. The *Gaayon Baayon* comes out from the *naamghar* reciting songs followed by the idol carriers, the Raja and the four officers. The *baaruwatis* take the *baaru* (shield) and by dancing and dancing go to the front side of the procession. In some areas, the *dhaal toruwal dhaaris* (bearers of shields and swords) perform *ronuondi* dance and advance forward. Behind them is a group who beats the *bordhul* to make the *baaruwatis* dance. In some areas the *dhaal toruwal dhaaris* take the *dhal toruwal* and the drum beats the *dhul dogora* and take the holy wooden structure from its assigned place to the open field. In different *melaas,* different *khuls* or clans beat the *bordhul*. In Baropujia area *melaa*, it is the privilege of the *Damlong* and *Pangchong* clan members only since ages past. The *paatidhul* is also beaten and by dancing and dancing another group advances. Behind them the *Satula Murti* of the Raja's house is taken. They are followed by *Gayon-Bayon* who beats the *dobaa*, (an instrument) *khool-nagera* (musical instruments) and move forward. Behind them the *Dekeraja* holds an umbrella under which the Raja goes. To his right is the *doloi* and other officials. At the end of the procession are the *ayotis* (women who sing) who go on singing devotional songs or *Hari Kirtan* all the way to the venue of the *mela*.

On the day of the *melaa*, the Raja and his officials are adorned with garlands made of *banamala* leaves. In the *patchoura,* the Raja is attired in traditional costumes and adorned with gold and silver ornaments by *Sunamati*.[25] Sandalwood paste mark is applied on the forehead. The significance of this is to ensure long life for the Raja.

In the early morning at the venue of the *melaa,* a small bamboo structure resembling a hut is constructed and banana leaves are placed on the top. To the east a raised earthen platform (*bedi*) is made and the *Saatula Murti* is placed on it. In some areas the idol is placed on a heap of banana leaves (front portion). In front of the idol three folds of banana leaves are kept. Here the public offers their oblations and donations and pay obeisance to the lord.[26] Whatever is collected (donations) is divided among the *pujaaris*, *Kunwaris* and the women who sing devotional songs. To the right of this raised earthen platform (*bedi*) sits the Raja and the *parishad barga* and for them a long raised earthen platform is made. To the right of the Raja, sits the *Dekarja* and to his left sits the *Doloi* – such is the custom. In front of the *Saatula Murti* there is *Gayon-Baayon* and the *aayotis* (women who sing) keep singing *naam prasanga*.

On direction of the *Dekaraja, dhaal* and *bet* (cane stick) are taken and some people engage in mock fight. At the end, the public collectively indulge in *haridhani* and the lord is again placed on the wooden structure to be brought back to its original place. This brings an end to the *melaa* and the Raja is again taken in a procession along with the *Satula Murti* and it is again placed in its assigned placed in the *naamghar*. Before it seven rounds are taken around the *naamghar*. Before they reach the *naamghar* they sing *ghunusaa* songs and they are obstructed by a group of people who asks them a few questions like 'why did the lord go out of the assigned place on that day' etc.[27]

When the questions have been answered, the way is cleared. This is a new addition. The Raja then treats all the people who accompanied him with food and after they have been treated, the *melaa* ends. It must be mentioned however that the rituals and social customs for holding these *melaas* differ from area to area.[28]

Barat Festival

The word *Barat* is a simpler form of the Assamese word 'Barat' which means penance or fasting. In order to appease God, fasting or *brat* is undertaken by a few girls or women and at the end of the fasting, a festival is arranged to culminate the occasion. This festival is called *Barat* and is celebrated by the plains Tiwas in the villages of Tetelia, Jerenga, Koroibari and Ajarbari of Morigaon district every year. These villages are considered to be traditionally sisters. The Tetelia village is *Borbhani* (eldest sister), Jerenga and Koroibari villages are *Majubhani* (middle sisters) and Ajarbari is the *Sarubhani* or youngest sister. A full moon day in the month of 'Push' (December/ January) or Magh (January/February) is generally chosen as the auspicious date for holding this festival.

Historical background

From the Tetelia Raja's family history it is evident that *brat* festival started from the time of Raja Ranasiddha Konwar.[29] Ronjoy Sing was installed as the first Raja of Tetelia. Being a youthful, handsome Raja, the Dimoria Raja is said to have given his daughter named Usha in marriage to him. He gave his second daughter to the Raja (chieftain) of Kumoi. The Dimoria Raja is said to have sent as dowry *Barat pujaa* with his daughters and advised his sons-in-law that if *Barat Pujaa* was held in their areas their states would be free from all kinds of dangers and the subjects would lead a life of peace and happiness. It appears that his advice was heeded accordingly and since then *Usha Barat* is celebrated by Tetelia Raja and *Bhada* or *Bhodia barat* was celebrated by Kumoi Raja. As the Kumoi Raja celebrated this *Barat* festival in the month of *Bhada* (August /September) this festival came to be known as *Bhadia Barat*. A few years after that, the Kumoi Raja celebrated this festival in the month of *Bohaag* (April-May) on Saturday, Sunday and Monday. But at present this has become almost extinct and the royal family of Kumoi has converted to

Neo-Vaishnavism and have become *Soru Koch*. Again, it is also said that the Kumoi Raja used to perform *Mal Gossain Pujaa* but he exchanged this *pujaa* with Dimoria Raja and took *Barat Pujaa* from him.

Adjacent to the Tetelia hills, at Tetelia the *Barat Pujaa* is held. There two *thaans* exist- *Kalikha thaan* and *Bongshi Badon thaan*. Prior to holding *Barat Pujaa*, *pujaa* must be offered at *Kalikha thaan.*[30] After this, *pujaa* must be offered to goddess Saraswati in the evening on *Kati Bihu* day which marks the formal beginning of the *Barat pujaa.*[31] For the *Saraswati pujaa*, a bunch of bananas, rice grains, flowers, sour fruits, betel nuts and leaves are required. The main participants of the *Barat pujaa* are four *aayotis* (ladies who sing) and one *Kunwari* who is called *brotheswari* or *borotoni*. After the *pujaas* are held for the *pujaa* is offered at *Kaalikaa thaan* for the main *Barat pujaa*. At *Kaalikaa thaan* tortoise, goat and other animals are sacrificed and the villagers who participate in the *pujaa* are present on the occasion and partake the flesh of the sacrificed animals along with other items and get ready for the *pujaa*[32].

The *broteshwari* is selected from a particular *kul*. If a young girl is not available in that particular '*Doloi vamsa*' then an old or middle aged woman may be selected as *broteshwari*. If she too is not available *borotoni* or *broteshwari* may be selected from other *Kuls*. From the day Saraswati *pujaa* is offered at *Kaalikaa thaan*, the *broteshwari* is given ritual bath with water collected from seven sources, after every seven days. The *broteshwari* as well as the four *aayotis* are to observe certain restrictions during *Barat Pujaa*.

According to the rituals, on the day preceding *Barat pujaa* a small hut is constructed in an east-west direction about four feet high, four feet length, four feet breadth and dry hay is placed on the top to act as a roof. This hut is called *Sungari (Kunwari)* hut. The responsibility of constructing this *Sungari* hut lies on the son of the Raja. The son carries out his responsibility with the co-operation of *Pator* and other officials by undertaking fast. The western side of the hut is left open for the *pujaa*. On the day of the *Barat pujaa* in the front side of the hut a trunk of banana tree (*kol bokhuwaar dingaa*) which resembles a boat is placed. Other rituals include weaving of cloth (which is required for the *pujaa*) in a single day by undertaking fast, *saat ghator pani tola*, (collecting water from seven ghats), *pujaas* to be offered to different deities like *Kalikha Devi, Kolia Gosai Burha Dangoria* and *Saraswati Devi*. On the day of the *Barat utsav* only in the presence of the Raja and his *parishad barga* can the *pujaa* be performed.

When everything is ready then in the middle portion of the *robha* in an eastern direction below a 'chondratap' (a canopy) on an earthen altar a *chaamor peera* (wooden piece used for sitting purpose) is placed and *Borotor Kunwari* is made to sit. Near the *Kunwari*, the *aayotis* sit and near the *aayoties aaisokol* (other women participants) take their seats. Near every *khuta* of the '*robha' dulas* are placed. At dusk on all sides '*Joor'* (a bunch of hay) tied together to a thick bamboo which resembles a torch are lighted to illuminate the area – lights and lamps are not used. To the accompaniment of the songs of the women the *Barat pujaa* begins. On that auspicious day, one hundred and twenty *adhayaay* songs are sung. When the first seven *aadhyay* songs are sung then with fire and burning cinders placed on a stick the dancers dance all around the *rabha* (temporary shed) once. The dancers with the sticks of burning cinders are called *Bhumura*. Since they dance all around the *robha* with fire it is called *Agnigarh*. Again as soon as the devotional songs are sung the *devataas* (divine beings) Lord Siva, (a human in the guise of the lord) arrives and along with Him comes his assistants – the demons, the *rakshyays*, bears, monkeys, tiger, deer, pig and various other animal mask wearing people who dance to the tune of the *paatidhool* (a kind of drum). The mask wearing people are called *nartaks*. It is then followed by other rituals such as *gorokhiya puja* and others. In the main *Barat* dance flocks of birds – *Telia Sareng, Kanua, Gurunda* and others made of cane and wood are made to dance to the tune of *paatidhool*.

All the *borotanis* and the a*ayotis* who undertake fasts take banana, rice grains, betel nuts and leaves from each *dula* and a small sum according to traditional ritual in the belief that they would live happily and peacefully. The flowers and flower garlands are then set afloat. The *borotani makes* a round of the entire *rabha* (a temporary shed).

After the fasting has been broken, the girls who undertake the fast get engaged in *pirajuj* (mock fight with one wooden *pira*). Before they take to *pirajuj* they take bath and wear dress made of *mugaa* silk

(*Pira* is a square or rectangular wooden object slightly raised above the ground with wood and *Juj* means fight). Four girls hold the *pira* and each with her own strength tries to pull it towards her side. The *aayotis* sprinkle basil leaves water on them from a *ghot (pitcher)*. While the *pirajuj* gets underway devotional songs are sung. The girl who succeeds in taking the *pira* to her side is rewarded with a gift by the Raja.

At the end, the *borotor kunwari* or *broteshwari* takes the *kekura dula* (curved sedan) and goes home singing devotional songs all the way. On that evening the villagers assemble and feast together.[33]

Hill Tiwa Festivals

The Tiwas living in Karbi-Anglong hill district celebrate a number of festivals throughout the year at different seasons. These festivals are *Sogra Missawa, Khelswaa Laṅgkhun Phuja, Yaangli, Waanswa* and *Maakro Missawa (Muinari Kanthi).*[34] The converted Christian Tiwas of this district celebrate Christmas, Easter, Good Friday, New Year's day, etc. Here a brief description is given of the traditional festivals that are celebrated in Tiwa dominated villages of Karbi-Anglong district. A noteworthy aspect is that though the names of the festivals are similar, the different *phoids* (*maahaars*) of the hill Tiwas follow their own customs and own tunes of their songs. The following festivals are celebrated by the different *phoids*.[35]

36. Marjong phoid – Waanswaa, Laangkhun phujaa, Sograa Missaawaa and Yaangli Missaawaa.
37. Aamsai phoid – Yaangli Missaawaa, Laangkhun Phujaa Missaawaa, Sograa Missaawaa.
38. Aamkha phoid – Wanswa Missaawaa, Phujaa Missaawaa, Sograa Missaawaa and Panthaai Salwaa.
39. Rongkhoi phoid – Yaangli Missaawaa and Langkhun Missaawaa
40. Aamni Phoid – Langkhun Missaawaa.
41. Maakro phoid – Maakro Khelswaa, Maakro Muinaari Kaanthi and Paanthai Salwaa.
42. Lumphoi phoid – Sograa Missaawaa.
43. Aamjong phoid – Sograa Missaawaa and Yaangli.

Sograa Missaawaa

Sograa Missaawaa is a popular hill Tiwa festival celebrated every year in the second week of the months of February and March when the *modaar simalu* flowers bloom. This festival is celebrated by the *Aamsai, Marjong, Lumphoi, Amri* and *Aamkha phoids* of Karbi Anglong district. As well as in a few border villages of Nowgaon and Morigaon inhabited mainly by Tiwas. While this festival goes on, no living being should be killed. If there are some who defy and still indulge in it the Tiwas believe that some misfortune may affect them and the society takes actions against such offenders. This festival starts on a Wednesday or Thursday and continues till Monday.

There are different folktales among the different *phoids* regarding celebration of this festival. According to *Aamsaiwali phoid*, an orphan boy named Maajibor who belonged to Sograa clan, one day saw a flower resembling cotton floating across the sky. Seeing the beautiful flower, he quickly collected a new piece of cloth and spread it out. Soon the flower fell on this piece of cloth. He then carefully wrapped it up with the cloth and took it home and showed it to the village officials - *loro, doloi, saot, aaji, phador, kay kamul, chaangdoloi, chaangmaji, suruma* and others. Impressed by the beautiful flower they assumed that it must be a boon sent by *Bala Khongor*, their lord and they named the flower 'Nasuni'. Taking that flower, as symbol they started celebrating *Sogra Missaawaa*. Since the boy belonged to *Sograa* clan, the festival came to be called *Sograa Missaawaa* (festival).

Though different *phoids* celebrate *Sogra Missaawaa,* there are differences in the customs they follow. Here, a description is given of how it is celebrated in Amswoi region, which is linked with Gobha Raja. Before the celebration of this festival on a Wednesday the village functionary designated as *phaador* goes to Gobha Raja's house along with two men from the general public and carry with them potatoes, arum, ginger, turmeric, etc along with a flute. When they reach the Raja's residence, they play flute in his courtyard and dance and give him the vegetables they carried along with them. They spend the night at the Raja's residence. The next day after getting the blessings of the Raja, they take with them Raja's *paguri* (head gear) and a bunch of betel nuts and go back to their village. They keep there the articles in the house of the *doloi*. The latter sacrifices a white cock in the honour and name of the Raja so that no untoward incident may happen. On Saturday, the flesh of the sacrificed bird is cooked alongwith *bahor khorisa* (bamboo shoot) and *samsuree* a kind of (jungle leaves). This is partaken by all the officials including *chaangdoloi* and *chaangmaji*. On Thursday, in the house of *phaikamul* (a village official) the villagers assemble and after taking rice beer go to pull out the *dol* (a variety of grass) from the water. The villagers get the *dol* and bring it to the village and then the *panthaais (*youths) with the beating of *khraam*, and playing of flutes like *paangsi* and *thuraang* send out a cat call. Then they place a bamboo mat in front of the courtyard of the *chaamaadi*. After sitting on the mat (*tokhra*) the *bor barikhaa* cuts the *dol* (i.e. grass or fodder meant for buffaloes) into a stipulated size and after squeezing it takes out the *mojja* (central portion). The squeezed out *mojja* is cut into one and one half metre size and fastened to a bamboo stick with thread. These look like bunches of flowers resembling *modaar* in bloom when tied together and are called *khum khaamti* or *phool khaati*. These *phool khaatis* are attached to the head gears or *paaguris* of three individuals. These three individuals adorned with *khumkhatis* are called *Tengore*, *Muthi Mosolong* and *Muthi mossawaa*. Besides them there is another person called 'puraa' who is adorned with a flower stick to his *paaguri* (head gear) and yet another adorned with branches of a tree on the *paaguri* which resembles that of deer horns, he resembles *mo'h* (buffaloes) or 'pahu' (deer). During the time of *Sograa misaawaa* dance, *khraam*, *paangsi* and *thuraang* musical instruments are used. The *puraa* or *buraa* dances first and behind him are the '*moh'* or deer and behind him the *Muthi mossaawaa* and *Muthi mosolong*. The three individuals adorned with *khumkhaati* are called *khamela*. Till the *sogra missawa* continues the *khamelas* cannot go home. Such is the traditional custom. That is why two male persons and two females are entrusted to cater to their needs including food. In addition to these *khamelas* four persons wear garment made of banana leaves which they call *sigaakhel* and move in the arena. This is done to avoid direct evil eyes on the *Sogra Missaawa* individuals.

Along with *khamelaaa, puraa and mosor* (deer) the *chaangdoloi*, *chaangmaji*, *surumaa* and other office bearers of the *chaamaadi* participate in the *Sograa missaawaa* dance. At first they dance in the courtyard of the *chaamaadi*. Then they go to the Gobha Raja's courtyard to dance. It is worth mentioning that there is a legend behind dancing in the Gobha Raja's courtyard. The Tiwas believe that the Gobha Raja's birth was at the source of 'River Killing' which is in the state of Meghalaya at Thin Maflang. From there the Gobha Raja is said to have come first to Amswoi where he set up a capital. In his memory a '*bheti*' still exists at *Amswoi*. Therefore to show due honour to him, soon after the *Sograa* dance at the *chaamaadi*, the people go to dance in the courtyard of the Gobha Raja. Only after that they can dance in the houses of the *loro, doloi, saot, maji, phador, phayakmul* and other office bearers according to traditional custom. They enter the *nubaar* and by singing in praise of *Nachuni* offer prayers to the presiding lord. At that time the housewife offers them *pohon mod* (rice beer) and *khaaji*. A noteworthy aspect of this dance is that there is no definite place or house where this dance is performed. Upto Sunday night, the dance is performed in the above mentioned houses. After this on Monday morning, the head gears which were worn are taken off and kept in the *chaamaadi*. On Tuesday, the *paanthaais* (young boys) take the betel nut bunches on their heads and go on dancing in the houses mentioned earlier and after it is all over, the musical instruments are kept back in the *chaamaadi*. In the second week on a Monday the *khumkhaati* and betel nut bunches are collected from the *chaamaadi* and by observing necessary customs are kept at *Sograasaal* or *sograasaalit*. This marks the end of *Sogra missawa* (festival).

Every year after harvesting operations are complete *phuja utsav* is celebrated by the hill Tiwas. On Tuesday every household of the village sacrifices a fowl for their welfare. This is done by the *borjelaa* at the *nubaar* after offering prayers.[44]

At the same time newly harvested rice, rice beer, *chira* (a variety of flattened rice), and other delicacies are offered. At night the *chaangdoloi, suruma, khuraamul* and other youths assemble in the *chaamaadi* (*dekachang*) and take blessings from the older generation. Then they take the *dhul* (drum), *baahi* (flute), *thurang* (flute) and to its rhythmical tunes sing and dance. From the *chaamaadi* they go and dance in the house of *deori, haadaari, baarika, chaangdoloi, surumaa* and all the houses in their village at night. At first they dance in the courtyard of a particular house for some time and then they enter the house. The housewife of the household makes prior arrangements for sitting and for drinking rice beer, *khaaji* water, etc. After partaking the offering, they sing and shower blessings in the following way:-

'O' syaagal syaagal

O' syokhuli, O' maakhuli

Ethado syaari khong tokhraanaa laung,

Khamlina lagong

Yaakasi karamaha takhana

Eyagraa kaaraamaaha takhana

Porse honga, pistase honga

O' syakhuli, o' maa' khuli

The English Translation briefly being

Eaten we have eaten, O' *aai* (mother), now we are leaving,

Heartful of boons we are showering

O' *aai* (mother) we are giving our blessings.

Laangkhun Phujaa

Laangkhun Phujaa or *Laangkhun Missawaa* is another popular festival of the Tiwas. This festival is celebrated every year in the months of *Aahin-Kati* (September/October/November). Except the *Maakro* and *Aamkha phoids* other *phoids* like *Raangkhoi*, Aamni, Aamri, Marjong etc, observe this festival.[45] The unique feature of this festival is that the members of the said *phoid* make *laangkhuns* and young girls and boys dance with them together. *Laangkhuns* are made from a variety of bamboo called *bijulee baah* (bamboo).[46] Leaving one and one half metre of a bamboo from the earth, the remaining portion is cut. The spaces between the joints are scraped finely and allowed to remain till the joint. At each of the joints therefore are bunches of finely scraped bamboo. These bamboos are called *laangkhuns*.[47] The *laangkhuns* are cut from a particular *Bijulee baah* grove on a pre-fixed day by village officials like *chaangdoloi chaangmaaji, suruma, loro, doloi* along with other villagers by observing traditional customs. From the particular bamboo grove from which *laangkhuns* would be made, rice beer is first offered and poured on the bamboo leaves from the gourd in the name of the mother of *Bijuleer baah* for appeasement so that she is not offended for being cut and does not cast any curses and nothing unfortunate happens. The number of *laangkhuns* should not exceed the required number and should not be less than twenty one.[48]

There are different folk tales behind observing this festival among the different *phoids* who celebrate this festival.[49] A description of a folk tale is given here which is prevalent among the *Aamni phoid*. According to their belief, once upon a time, *Burha Ramsa* the chief deity did not get any share of sacrifice anywhere and so he created a lot of scarcity in this *phoid* as a consequence of which the members could not even collect a handful to eat. Not getting to eat they descended to the plains. But in the plains too they did not get to eat even by begging. A woman amongst them then sold her child to a rich family in Silchang area in exchange for a handful of rice. One day *Burha Ramsaa* showed a dream to one Sogrolublai belonging to *Hong-gam* clan that only if he gets a share of sacrifice and observes *laangkhun phujaa* customs then scarcity and famine would disappear.[50] But the questions arose as to how to observe the *laangkhun phujaa*. Since a large quantity of rice would be required to make rice beer and who would bear the expenses as they were only living hand to mouth. To this *Burha Ramsaa* replied that for preparation of rice beer, rice or paddy was not required. Instead, the leaves of the *aamlokhi* (*emblic* myrobalan) should be placed in an empty gourdshell which would act as *baakhor* (yeast) for the beer and that he would be satisfied with it. Sogrolublaik was thus made to understand. That is why even today the aamni *phoid* members say that it is the traditional custom of *Burha Ramsaa*.[51]

Yaangli Missawaa or Lakshmi Pujaa

Every five or six years the hill Tiwas of *Maarjong, Aamsoi, Rongkhai* and *Maagro phoids* celebrate *Yaangli Missawa* (festival)[52]. This festival begins on a Wednesday in the month of *Cho't* (March-April). Sacrifices are made in the honour of Goddess Lakshmi with ducks, pigeons, hens, goats, rice, rice beer and other articles[53]. To meet the expenses the *loro, deuri, saot, maaji* and other officials of Barmarjong collect donations from each family from their branch villages.[54] A part of the sacrifice is offered in the assigned place called *yaanglisaal*.[55] From the time the sacrifice starts till the end, dancing continues with *dhaal* and *toruwaal* (*sword*). The object behind this is to see that no evil may capture Goddess *Lakshmi*. After a part of the sacrifice has been offered at the *yaanglisaal,* the dancers come in a dancing manner with one black goat whose ear is twisted and in a crying manner is taken to the house of the *Loro*. Rice powder mixed with water is sprinkled on all the people who come from the *yaanglisaal* to the *Loro's* house. If anybody steps on this water, it is considered an insult to goddess Lakshmi.[56] In the *Loro's* house again to satisfy goddess Lakshmi, the black goat which was brought from the *yaanglisaal* is sacrificed according to rituals. Dances continue with the beating of drums. It is worth mentioning that there are no songs sung during this festival. Instead prayers are recited for goddess Lakshmi.[57]

There is a folk tale prevalent amongst the Tiwas behind the observance of this festival.[58] They believe that Lord Siva once had discussion with *Chaari Bhai* regarding the eatables on which the human beings could survive and during discussion it came to light that by consuming roots and potatoes alone hunger could not be satisfied. Therefore a meeting was convened in heaven in which all the gods and goddesses were present to discuss the problem. It was at this meeting that Lord Siva proposed the name of Goddess Lakshmi. Again a problem arose as to how to bring Goddess Lakshmi from the midst of the ocean where she lives. Then it was decided to send the Tuni bird to fetch her. After flying to the place where goddess Lakshmi lived the Tuni bird filled her appetite and went back without taking goddess Lakshmi. When she reported back *Chaari Bhai* was furious and in his wrath gave the bird two slaps, as a result of which his two cheeks became black.[59] At last it was decided to send a rat to fetch goddess Lakshmi. To accompany the rat an army equipped with *dhaal*, *toruwaal* was sent. While going through the waters the *rakshyas* in the guise of big fish like *row*, *borali* made unsuccessful attempts to capture the boat, However, braving all odds, the army managed to reach the place, where goddess Lakshmi resided[60]. The rat narrated the details as to why they had gone to fetch her. Though she was initially reluctant to come, she ultimately agreed as it was the direction of Lord Siva. She however set some conditions for her visit and this was that ducks, pigeons and goats should be sacrificed in her honour. When this was agreed upon, goddess Lakshmi emerged from the ocean and the army that was sent helped to place her in the boat. Along with her the ginger, turmeric, arum, corn and others also got into the boat. To commemorte this event the Tiwas celebrate *yaangli* festival every five or six years.

Waanswaa Festival

Every five years, the *Aamkhawali phoid* of the Tiwas celebrate *Waanswaa* which is their main festival. *Waanswa* means *pithaguri* (rice powder) *khunda* (grind) festival. It is also called *Sotonga* and *Maldeo Raja's utsav*.[61] This festival is observed in the months of June/July and begins on a Tuesday evening and continues till the night of Thursday. The main festival is held on Wednesday. This festival is celebrated under the leadership of *chaangdoloi*, *chaangmaaji*, *suruma*, *khuraamul khuraasaa* and others. In whichever village this festival is hosted, the youths (boys) belonging to the same *phoid* of that village go to the different villages to invite the youths of their *phoid* to their festival. The invited youths reach that village on Tuesday evening and keep singing and dancing till the end of the festival.[62] Those few days each house of the village takes care of their food. On Wednesday morning in the courtyard of the *chaangdoloi,* the *uraals* (wooden object which is hollow at the middle portion) are placed in a circular manner. At the stipulated time, the youths of the different villages following their customs and rituals take sticks (*uraal mari*) in their hands and start grinding the wet rice in the *uraals* (hollow wooden object) till they are fine by dancing to the beats and tunes of *khraam* and *paangsi*. In this manner they are to grind about ten to twelve mounds of rice grains. The atmosphere wears a festive look and people attired in their traditional best are the onlookers. Later on, the fine rice powder is distributed among all the houses and they steam the quota given to them. All this is collected and deposited in the house of *chaangdoloi*. At night they assemble again at the *chaangdoloi's* home courtyard and offer the steamed rice powder in the name of

Sotanga Raja, Maldeo Raja and their ancestors and then they consume themselves.[63]

The *Aamkha phoid* celebrates this festival in a unique way. The youths who come from different villages collect the names of the local village belles from the elders of the village where the festival is held and sing songs entangling them.[64] It is through these songs that eligible bachelors try to find their life partners. But they see to it that such songs are not meant for the *belles* of their own clan, as marriage within the same clan is taboo in Tiwa society. While the *wanswa* dance goes on, most of the *panthais* (youths) take weaving instruments like *jotor* and *chereki* (weaving instruments), and agricultural products like corn, cucumber, *bangi*, pineapple etc, in their hands to attract their beloved (girls who come to witness the festival or the local belles) and give vent to their expression through songs.[65] The objective of taking the weaving instruments etc, imply that they are in need of a girl who can weave.[66] The agricultural products in their hands are symbols of productivity. Many enter into wedlock after enjoying this festival. Prospective bride's mothers also keep ready a pot full of rice beer in anticipation that they may get a prospective groom. During this festival, new office bearers of the *chaamaadi* are advised by the outgoing office bearers – *chaangdoloi, chaangmaji, suruma, khurasa, khuramul* not to discard their traditional customs but to continue with the traditions year after year as given by *Lampha Raja*, *Sotonga Raja* and *Maldeo Raja*. The *khoraalas* (village damsels) clad in their best take the *daarun* (*Zu* server) and serve *Zu* to all. After this ritual is over they dance again and by singing and dancing they spend the night. On Friday morning all the invited *panthais* (youths) are entertained with due honour and bid adieu.

There is a folk tale behind observance of this festival. According to this folktale, there once lived a husband and wife duo by the names of Rampha and Ramma.[67] Overcome with hunger they became lean and thin. They therefore wondered what to eat in order to survive. They took this problem to Sotonga Raja and Maldeo Raja. Seeing both the Sotonga Raja and Maldeo Raja in good health, the duo were taken aback. What were the edibles that they could have possibly taken to have such robust health, were the questions that haunted them. Ultimately they were advised by them to take roots to satisfy their hunger. They did accordingly but that could not satisfy their hunger.

Again they went to Sotonga Raja and Maldeo Raja. This time they were told to dig out the potatoes for consumption. This too had no effect. At last, the two Rajas advised them to take rice and this only could satisfy their hunger. Both Rampha and Ramma, then concluded that rice was the commodity by which Sotonga Raja and Maldeo Raja kept good health. From that time onwards both Rampha and Ramma advised human beings to take rice for survival. Such is the belief of the hill Tiwas.

According to another folk tale, once upon a time, twelve *deos* and twelve *devees* (divine being) started cultivations of crops in various parts of the earth. Starting from Seraseri, the other cultivated areas included Wasiwari, Khorafoda, Borsira, Borlemphra, Maathaalbar, Mathaalpisa, Makha Koja, Makha Khojom, Borthal, Soruthal, Borkholong and other places. Cultivation was undertaken continoulsy for twelve years but there was no production. At last it was decided to seek help from human beings. When cultivation began in unison with human beings, there was a lot of production. The divine beings then showered the human beings with blessings that henceforth human beings should depend on cultivation for survival.

With the abundance of food grains at their disposal twelve youths and twelve damsels wondered what to do. After discussion a bright idea struck them and this was celebration by way of festival. But before celebration, the traditional *chaamaadi* was to be constructed. For construction of *chaamaadi* again instruments like *dao, axe* etc., were required. So, on a fixed day, the *Chaamaadi* officials, *chaangdoloi, chaangmaaji* and suruma went together to the blacksmith taking with them a gourdful of rice beer to request him to make the implements required to construct *chaamaadi*. The blacksmith accepted the gift and soon made the required implements. Then three Tuesdays and three Wednesday's were fixed for construction of *chaamaadi*. Rice beer required for those day was also kept ready. Then began the construction of the *chaamaadi* and after completion they organised songs and dances. The *chaangdoloi, chaangmaji, suruma* and other officials after discussions took the decision of celebrating *waanswaa* festival and for that a large quantity of rice beer was prepared. They also felt that to add to their enjoyment *the chaangdoloi, chaangmaaji, suruma* and other village officials of other village must be invited. That tradition therefore continues to this day.

Muinari Kaanthi Missaawaa

Amongst the *Maakrowaali Phoid* of the Tiwas the *Maakro Missaawaa* or *Muinaari Kaanthi Missaawaa* is the most attractive of all their folk dances. Generally in the hill Tiwa folk dances, the women do not participate but in this folk dance women participation is essential. Similar to the *nimsokirung* dance of the Karbis, in this dance too, the Tiwa damsels go in between boys and dance. But before they dance, it is necessary is find out the *kul* or clans of the boys, as such dance induces romance and may end up in marriage. Marriage in Tiwa community is forbidden if the girl and boy belong to the same clan as stated earlier. Generally in other folk dances the instruments used are *Khraam*, *paangsi*, *thuraang,* etc, but in this particular folk dance *tumding*, *tagar* and *muhuri* instruments are used. With these three instruments the young Tiwa boys and girls dance to their tune in a serpentine manner.

A few lines of a song sung along with this dance –

'Loro nona likaido, loro lore li

Doloi nona likaido, toli toli li

Majisnes nona likaido, maaja maajaa li

Sangote nona likaido, songe songe li

kurfang duwar fang, prune khusumang

Aaro'syamsa phiwana, somod pasewang[73]

The English translation being

If you go to the Loro's house, go running

If you go to the Doloi's house go in group

If you go to the Maaji's house go in between

If you go to the Saot's house ask and ask and go

But if I come again

I will ask for a relationship.

The folk dances of the Tiwas are associated with festivals. Amongst the *Maakro phoid* too, there is a folk festival which is celebrated every five or six years in the *Phaad Magro* village of Meghalaya.[74] Their branch villages are Ulukunchi, Silaguri, Kromkunchi and Khumrai Khora of Aamri *Mouza* in Hamren sub-division. During the festival it is obligatory on the people of these villages to participate[75]. This festival begins on a Wednesday and continues till the night of Friday in the house of the *Loro*.

There is a folk tale behind observance of this festival. The chief deity of *Maakgrowali phoid* is *Kablaa*[76]. The unique characteristic of this deity is that it takes offerings on the western side unlike the other deities who accept offerings on the eastern side. The other *phoids* therefore have a fear psychosis about this deity. According to their folk tale, once it happened that *Kabla* deity did not get a share of *pujaa* sacrifice anywhere and hence he made His appearance in the form of a human being at the house of a widow and asked for shelter and food. Though the widow was able to provide shelter, she could not provide food as she could not afford. *Kabla* deity then revealed his identity and told her that if sacrifice was given to him then her poverty would vanish and a festive atmosphere would prevail with song and dances. The widow then agreed. As soon as she agreed her house became full of wealth and paddy and from the heaven suddenly, young boys and damsels, playing the *tumding, tagor* and *muhuri* descended in her house and throughout the night dances and songs were performed. In this way only at nights, songs and dances were performed. The widow belonged to *Soleng kul* and her *kul* (clan) has been given recognition as Loro Kul.[77]

On another day, a man belonging to *Maaslai Kul* not getting to eat went in search of wild potatoes to the jungles, but did not get any. While returning back he lost his way and in a distant happened to see some light. Seeing the light he proceeded and reached the house of the widow. He then enquired from her if he could spend the night there but she refused as she did not have anything to offer him for the night. But the man insisted only for shelter for that particular night and she agreed.[78]

At night as usual in the widow's house, *Kabla devata* sent *tumding, tagor, muhuri, dhool*, and song, dances began. The man who belonged to Maaslai kul was astonished to see the un-natural scenes and came to know that it was the activities of *Kabla devata.* He then came back to his village and narrated everything to his fellow villagers who agreed to accept *Kabla devata* as their chief deity and they follow the rituals necessary in his honour even to this day. The house of the widow where *Kabla devata* had taken shelter in Phaad Magro village of Meghalaya. The person who belonged to *Maaslai kul* and who saw the supernatural dance of *Kabla* was a resident of the branch village of Phaad Magro. That is why every five or six years the old and young alike have a get together and participate in this festival after contributing collectively.

The folk songs of Tiwa society are associated with their festivals[79]. *The folk songs* can be divided into four divisions:

(a) festival based songs (b) love based songs

(c) agricultural labour songs (d) folk tale based songs

The *festival based songs* are :

(a) Sogra Missawaa (b) Wanswaa Missawaa

(c) Khelswaa Missawaa (d) Laangkhun Phuja Misswaa

(e) Magro Khelssawa Missawaa (f) Muinare Missawaa and Barat utsav songs

The *love based songs* are:

(a) Panthai Khorala or Somoda rojawaa geet

The *agricultural labour* songs are:

(a) Panthai solwa geet

(b) Mai rawa geet

(c) Mai pothala geet

(d) Phaadaar Kasewa geet

Folk tale songs are :

(a) Uwaan Suwaa Phaadon Sikaaya geet

(b) Chaamaadi Saangtuwaa geet

NOTES AND REFERENCES

1. TS, p. 45.
2. Field study, informant – Rimol Amsi.
3. LST, pp. 98-99.
4. *Ibid*, p. 97.
5. *Ibid*.
6. Senapati, G.C, *Tiwa (Lalung) Janajaatir Bihu*, Thuraang, 2002, p. 32.
7. TS, p. 95.
8. *Loc cit*, p. 33.
9. *Ibid*.
10. *Ibid*., p. 34.
11. *Ibid*.,
12. *Ibid*., p. 35.
13. *Ibid*., p. 36.
14. *Ibid*., p. 37.
15. *Ibid*., p. 38.
16. *Ibid*., p. 39.
17. RRK, p. 48.
18. *Ibid*.
19. *Ibid*.
20. *Ibid*., p.49.
21. TSRG, pp. 135-136.
22. RRK, p.135.
23. *Ibid*, p. 51.
24. *Ibid*, p. 52.
25. *Ibid*.
26. *Ibid*, p. 53.
27. *Ibid*.

28. *Ibid.*, p. 57.
29. TSRG, Part I.
30. RRK, p. 57.
31. *Ibid.*
32. *Ibid.*
33. *Ibid*, p. 60.
34. Pator M, 'Tiwa Sakalor Jaatiya Utsav Paarbon', *(Sangkhorla)*, p. 51.
35. *Ibid*, p. 53.
36. Pator, M.ed., *Phera*, *Tiwa Mathonlai Tokhra*, 2000, Jagiroad, p.6.
37. *Loc.cit,* p. 50.
38. *Phera*, p.14.
39. *Ibid.*
40. *Ibid*, pp. 6-7.
41. *Ibid*, p.7.
42. Field study, informant, Maheswar Pator.
43. *Phera*, p.7.
44. *Loc.cit,* p. 50.
45. *Phera*, p.14.
46. *Ibid.*
47. *Ibid.*
48. *Ibid.*
49. *Ibid.*
50. *Ibid.*
51. *Ibid*, p.15.
52. *Loc.cit,* p. 51.
53. *Ibid.*
54. *Ibid.*
55. *Ibid.*

56. *Ibid.*
57. *Ibid.*
58. *Phera* p.16.
59. *Phera*, p.17.
60. *Ibid.*, p.1.
61. *Loc.cit.*, p. 52.
62. *Ibid.*
63. *Ibid.*
64. *Ibid.*
65. *Ibid.*
66. *Ibid*, p. 52.
67. *Phera*, pp.1-2.
68. *Ibid*, p. 2.
69. *Ibid*, p. 3.
70. *Ibid*, p. 4.
71. *Loc.cit,* p.51.
72. *Ibid.*
73. *Ibid*, p. 52.
74. *Phera,* p.11.
75. *Ibid.*
76. *Ibid*, p.12.
77. *Ibid.*
78. *Ibid*, p. 13.
79. *Ibid*, p. 53.

6

Conclusion

The Tiwas are a small tribal community with egalitarian ethos and represent a dense close knit form of unity. They inhabit the plains and hills of Assam and Meghalaya and are called plains Tiwas and hill Tiwas according to their area of settlement and social structure. They are a branch of the Bodo group and are ethnically of Mongoloid origin. They belong to the Tibeto-Burman group of languages of the Sino-Tibetan speech family. They are believed to have migrated in the remote past by different routes. They are rich in oral literature, comprising of myths, tales, legends, proverbs, songs and riddles.

There are several legends prevalent among them regarding their migration and origin of the names of their tribe, Lalung and Tiwa. Their early history is shrouded in myths and legends. There were some groups of Tiwas who were settled by the Jayantia Raja in his territory and those principalities were Gobha, Nellie, Khola and Sahari. The Jayantia Buranjis do not mention the exact date of their establishment but the Ahom officials called them *dantiyolia* because they lived in the *danti* (meaning border) areas or periphery of the Ahom kindgdom. During the medieval period, groups of Tiwas migrated from Jayantia territory to Ahom Kingdom for several reasons. The migration and formal settlement took place during the reign of Ahom king Jayadhvaj Singh (1648-63) after negotiations. This led to the establishment of five and seven principalities or vassal states of the Tiwas and their chieftians were called *Paacho Rajas* and *Saato Rajas* respectively in the history of Assam. The chiefs of these principalities paid taxes to the Ahom Government and assisted them with their men when required and there was a degree of subordination too.

During the time of the Ahom-Mughal wars when Pratap Singh was the Ahom king, the chiefs of the Tiwa principalities of Gobha, Nellie and Khola who were under the tutelage of the Jayantias went over to the Ahom King and sought their protection. The Ahom king is said to have responded favourably to them. This led to the displeasure of the Jayantia king who was waiting for an opportunity to get them back. During the reign of the Ahom King Jayadhvaj Singh (1648-63), the Jayantia king sent envoys felicitating him on his assumption of the royal office together with a request seeking the return of the Tiwa principalities of Gobha, Nellie and Khola from the Ahom king. On refusal, relations between the Ahoms and the Jayantias become strained. During the days of the Ahom king Rudra Singh (1714-44) these three principalities came back under the Jayantias again but the date and circumstances of their return have not been recorded in the *Jayantiya Buranji* or any other chronicles of the period.

They Tiwa chief tairfs rendered timely assistance is various expeditions of the Ahom kings. Though on most occasions they were loyal, during the later part of the Moamaria uprising, they switched over sides and joined hands with the rebels. This antagonised the Ahom kings who took punitive action against them. The intervention of the East India Company by the forces of Captain Welsh led to suppression of the Moamaria uprisings. During Burmese invasion of 1817, 1819 and 1821 the people of Assam including the Tiwas suffered from the atrocities perpetrated on them. The Anglo-Burmese War of 1824 led to the victory of the British and defeat of the Burmese. With the advent of British rule, all the Tiwa principalities suffered extinction yet, descendants of the chiefs of these principalities are still addressed by the Tiwas as Rajas and they are considered as socio-religions heads in their respective areas. During festive occasions they adorn their traditional dress. Troubles between the Tiwas and the British arose over the increased amount of taxation, and the order banning the cultivation of poppy. The highhandedness of the Deputy Commissioner Lieutenant Herbert Sconce ultimately erupted in an uprising called popularly as Phulaguri Dhawa of 1861. It was in this uprising that the Tiwas confronted the British and many lost their lives.

The Phulaguri upsurge left bitter memories and the discontentment against alien rule continued. While the British were looking out for fresh avenues of revenue, the discontentment against their rule took the form of various movements. Ultimately in 1947 the British handed over the power and India became independent. Several thousand Indians lost their lives in the struggle for freedom including many Tiwas.

Change is inevitable in society though every society may have its own eco-system. Progress in science and technology, education, religion, development in socio-economic spheres, demographic changes, widening of communication networks are some of the catalysts of the processes of social change. Along with the rest of India, the tribal societies of the North-East too have experienced social, economic, cultural and political changes in the 1990's and globalisation has begun to leave its impact.

Assertion of distinct identities both regional and ethnic are major issues in the socio-political life in contemporary India. The twin concepts of majority and minority have complicated matters and democratic politics are more afflicted by this majoritan-minoritan cleavage. In India ethnic movements in the North-east are necessarily minority movements based on ethnic identity and assertion of their rights as ethnic minorities. The upsurge in ethno nationalism in recent decades has resulted in frequent *bandhs*, conflicts and violence. This may be due to the fact that the existing political establishments have not been able to manage their contradictions and have failed to accommodate ethnic aspirations. The problem of ethnic upsurges, conflicts and violence may also be partly attributed to accelerated pace of modernisation leading to struggle for power and resources and partly due to forces unleashed by the processes of globalisation producing uneven economic development or regional imbalances and deprivation. Scholars have argued that survival in a plural society is possible by providing space to diversity and attempts at levelling it produces hatred and bitterness. Recognition of the right to personal autonomy and group identity is essential to ensure that the principles of self determination, participation and tolerance are allowed to flourish. In modern times, an ethnic group can assert itself successfully only when it asserts itself as an organised political entity. Hence the yearning for political autonomy.

The Tiwas who constitute an ethnic group of this region have been drawing national attention to their demands. As early as 1928 the Kachari community comprising of Rabhas, the Sonowals, the Meches, the Thengals, the Lalungs, the Saranias, etc. were raising demands for reservation of seats to the elected bodies. The plains tribes of Assam including the Lalungs got four seats reserved for them as a result of the Simon Commission's recommendations.

In the first ministry formed in Assam by Mohammad Saadula, no member belonged to the plains tribes. When the Saadula ministry resigned and Gopi Nath Bordoloi formed the ministry, the representatives of the Tiwas were included. Bordoloi championed the cause of the tribals by demanding creation of tribal belts and included for the first time Roop Nath Brahma a plains tribal in his ministry. When the Civil Disobedience Movement began, Bordoloi Ministry resigned and Saadula again formed the Government. The Saadula Government's land policy was severely criticized by the tribal leaders in the fifth session of the All Assam Tribal League held at Mangoldoi in 1945. Bordoloi took advantage of the situation, formed the Government and proposed reservation of seats for plains tribal along with some other concessions. In March 1947, the All Assam Tribal League submitted a memorandum to the Constituent Assembly demanding creation of Scheduled areas in the plains of Assam under the Fifth Schedule to the Constitution.

The demands of the plains tribals in Assam did not receive much attention during the period of Indian Independence. The sub-committees constituted for the purpose considered the population of the plains tribal as being gradually assimilated with the population of the plains and recommended that this population be treated as a minority. There were further suggestions that the matters relating to their representation and protection of their land would be considered by the minorities sub-committee.

With new immigrants entering the state, provision was made for the creation of tribal belts and blocks in Assam and prohibition of transfer of land belonging to the tribal and other protected classes within these belts and blocks. The British administration devised the line system in 1916 and adopted it in 1920 to thwart un-authorised occupation of land. The concept of tribal belts and blocks was evolved in 1939 and incorporated in a 1945 resolution.

After the Independence, the All Assam Tribal Youth League which included representatives of the Tiwas submitted a memorandum to the Prime Minister in 1978 on the problems faced by the indigenous tribal population. The Tiwa Students Union, Nowgong also submitted a memorandum on 4th September, 1991 and again on 30th January, 1992.

The Tiwas through their forum the Lalung Darbar and the Lalung Youth Front have been demanding creation of an autonomous district within Assam since 1967. Another organisation, the All Assam Tiwa Students Union too supported this demand.

On 10th May 1993, the Autonomous Lalung District Demand Committee submitted a memorandum to the Chief Minister of Assam for creation of an Autonomous Lalung District Council for the Tiwas. On 17th September, 1993 the All Assam Tiwa Students Union further reiterated its demand. The Memorandum contained historical background, a map of the proposed autonomous district etc.

On 10th November 1993, the Government of Assam held discussions with the members of the Autonomous Lalung District Demand Committee. This Committee submitted another Memorandum on 18th November 1993 for autonomy to the Lalungs.

Demand for creation of a Tiwa Autonomous district under the provisions of the Sixth Schedule of the Constitution of India, was made by All Tiwa Student's Union, the All Tiwa Women Association, the Tiwa Cultural Society and the Tiwa Sahitya Sabha in December 1993 together with recognition of Tiwa language and its introduction in Roman script at the primary level as a vernacular subject. The Government of Assam set-up a committee to weigh the pros and cons to grant autonomy in the areas inhabited by them. On 27th May 1994 the All Tiwa Students Union again submitted a Memorandum for grant of autonomy to the Tiwas.

Based on the Memorandum of Settlement, the Government of Assam promulgated on 13th July, 1995, the Lalung (Tiwa) Autonomous Council Ordinance, 1995. An interim Lalung Autonomous Council was set up on 25th July, 1995 at Morigaon district. Its responsibility is to look after the village councils.

The traditional Tiwa society has been undergoing change like other societies due to various influences. Yet despite these changes there have been elements of continuity. Of the social institutions family has been in continuity though it has changed from joint to nuclear type. At the macro level, people still continue to be governed by the village organisation, *borkhel bichaar*, taboos, rites and rituals, customary modes of behaviour, with social structures still tightly knit. The Tiwa culture is both collective and participatory however when the cultural elements get altered they carry with them the earlier features in modified forms. Although the traditional forms are still in practice, there is a chance that these forms may altogether disappear, along with their practitioners. If there is development, if education and job opportunities are provided it cannot be expected that the people would remain where they are, at the folklore level. As a result of the influence from other communities, the traditional youth dormitory called *Chaamaadi* has withered away in the plains. The young boys no longer spend their working and sleeping hours in the dormitory but go to school like the boys of the neighbouring areas. The *Chaamaadi* which is of indigenous architectural style is used for community discussions only. This is also the case in some of the hill Tiwa villages, where Christian missionaries encourage young boys to go to school. In a few villages, however, the dormitory system continues to exist.

As far as construction of house is concerned people still collect their building materials almost wholly from the forest or jungle nearby. Though thatch is mainly used, the affluent among them, though few in number have gone for corrugated iron sheets as roof and the elite among them have re-inforced concrete cement houses with all the paraphernalia of a modern house. Socio-religious functions are still practised by the people but these days it is according to one's economic capacity and the time that he could devote. The traditional houses in the hill villages do not have windows but the houses of the converted Christians have windows.

Agriculture is still the main economic activity and the majority among them are cultivators. Rice is their staple food and rice beer is still taken by them and it forms an indispensable part of their socio religious ceremonies. As regards the clothes they attire, they still wear the dhoti in plains villages like their counterparts belonging to other communities. But these days, they also wear trousers and shirts if they can afford. They however see to it that each of them possesses a *tagla* or their traditional waist coat which is a mark of their identity and generally worn on festive occasions. The traditional dress of plains Tiwa women is *mekhela chaddar* like the neighbouing people. As far as the hill Tiwa men are concerned they continue to wear a piece of loin cloth on the lower portion just to cover their private parts. The educated among them and those who have got jobs prefer to use trousers and shirts. Women continue to wear the traditional dress of blouse for the upper part and a thick piece of cloth tied to the waist, covering the legs but girls have started wearing *salwar kameej* like their counterparts in Assam and northern India. They still cling to their clan system. Though women empowerment is a contemporary Pan-Indian issue, both hill and plains Tiwas women appear to remain content with the household as their domain. They still do not have a voice in their respective village councils. Females are debarred entry to *chaamaadi* or youth dormitory. However, unlike the pan India scenario, women in Tiwa society are still unperturbed by their menfolk regarding dowry.

Changes in their traditional society have been noticed with the advent of Neo-Vaishnavism/Hinduism in the plains and Christianity in the hills as stated earlier. When Sankardeva (1449-1568) preached Neo-Vaishnavism he succeeded in swaying the emotions of the people including the Tiwas. Many amongst the Tiwas then gave up their traditional religion and embraced Vaishnavism, some even adopted titles of Koch community for elevation, the process being called Sanskritisation. They then offered prayers at *naamghars*, gave up their *kul* (clan) system. A rupture thus seems to have permeated their society and this led to a change in the Tiwa world view as they got assimilated in the Assamese society.

The advent of Christianity brought a change in the traditional society of the hill Tiwas. The converts would often consider their previous way of life as old fashioned and that it had no relevance with their present day living. The humanitarian work of missionary doctors and nurses gave an added charm to the religious teachings. Many started discarding their previous way of life. Many attended the schools started by these missionaries and in the process they got educated and can now converse well in English. They gave up their traditional religion and traditional way of living.

Major Findings

1. The principalities or vassal states of the Tiwas no doubt faced extinction during British rule but these specified areas still exist with their former names and the descendants of the chiefs are still looked upon as Rajas and given honour in their respective areas by the Tiwas.
2. The Tiwas have been given the status of Scheduled Tribe (Plains) but their counterparts settled in the hill district of Karbi-Anglong and Ri-Bhoi district of Meghalaya are yet to get the status of Schedule Tribe (Hills). As such they have been deprived of many facilities.
3. Assimilation and acculturation through Neo-Vaishnavism/ Hinduism and Christianity have occurred amongst the plains Tiwas and hill Tiwas. Many among the plains Tiwas who have adopted Koch surnames do not like to reveal their Tiwa identity. Similarly in Meghalaya many, Tiwas have been converted to Christianity and they prefer to be identified as Khasis.
4. Though the Tiwas have been demanding an Autonomous district they have been given an interim Autonomous District Council with no demarcation of areas. As such they are still yearning for political autonomy in the areas where they are in a majority.
5. Despite the changes going on, the Tiwas have still been maintaining some of their traditional rites, festivals, customary laws, religious beliefs and costumes. The Joon Beel Melaa is still held annually where they carry on the trade through the traditional barter system. There are many additions these days- wooden furniture is sold here in a large scale, vegetable vendors and others bring their goods in the hope that they would get sold fast as many people visit the fair. Their trade however is with money.

The Tiwas are still socially and economically backward. The percentage of literacy among them is very low and they hardly think of women empowerment. They appear to be contented with the traditional agricultural life and only a few are interested in trades and professions.

Glossary of Vernacular Terms

Aabi	Grandmother
Adhyaay	A chapter, a section
Aahaar	The third month of the Hindu Year, generally corresponding to June 16 to July 15.
Aahin	The sixth month of the Hindu year, generally corresponding to September 16 to October 15.
Aaja	Grandfather
Aakhai	Puffed rice grain, an edible item.
Aahoi Lowa	Welcoming Goddess Lakshmi by bringing the first harvested crop with a song.
Aam	Raised bamboo platform to dry leaves in hill Tiwa villages.
Aardhara	An official of the Tiwa Raja whose duty was to protect him from sun, rain etc.
Aarkura	Cutting the jungles and making the land fit for cultivation purposes.
Aaroiya	Dried fish used in preparation of *sukati*, which is not finely ground.
Aaroiya Sewa	Term used in *Raati Sewaa* occasion, when only a fowl is sacrificed.
Aayotis	Women who sing devotional songs.
Agnigarh	The wall of fire surrounding the city of Usha.
Akaari	Uncleaned and broken rice grains.
Aai Gossani	Deity of the Tiwas.
Aus gaaraa	A ceremony performed after the birth of a child. It is also called *manshwa*.

Aahu	A variety of paddy.
Amsih	Surname of hill Tiwa.
Auniati Gosain	The head of the *Auniati Satra.*
Asaraniya	Non Vaishnavites.
Baakhor	A circular shaped indigenous yeast made of a variety of edible leaves and grounded rice grains used in making traditional rice beer.
Baagh Raja	Lord of the jungle.
Baalaa Khongor	Deity
Baaro	Twelve
Banamalaa	A variety of leaf used for religious purposes.
Bangkuaa	Alone
Barat	Penance or fasting.
Baao	A variety of paddy sown broadcast in spring.
Barghar	A sacred placed of the Tiwas.
Barikhaa	A village messenger.
Barkabir	Brother-in-law
Baaruati	A shieldsman
Basanti puja	*Durga Pujaa* performed in the spring season.
Baayu	Wind
Bedi	A raised earthen platform.
Bet	Cane
Bhaada	The fifth month of the Hindu year generally corresponding to August 16 to September 15.
Bhaandaari Khel	A part of *buraakhel* entrusted with the responsibility of supplying betel nuts and rice beer during festive occasions.
Bhaang	A kind of drug
Bhaar	A basket with various commodities in it like rice cakes, betel nuts etc.
Bhagabati	Deity

Bhelaaghar	A temporary hut of straw, dried plantain leaves, etc. made by the youths for feasting on the night before *Magh Bihu.*
Bheti Bhaar	A number of commodities offered by the villagers to their chief, the Raja, on festive occasions mostly on *Bohaag Bihu.*
Bhitor Maaji	Official who looked after the needs of the Raja and his officials when a *Raj Sabha* was convened.
Bichaarmaaji	Chief Judge
Bihu Kormi	Lord of the agricultural implements.
Bihuwaan	A woven Assamese towel.
Biriya	A piece of split bamboo used in carrying bundles of paddy on the shoulder.
Bichu	Bihu
Boisaak	The first month of the Hindu calendar corresponding to April 15 to May 16.
Borbarikhaa	Head of the village messengers.
Borbhani	Eldest sister
Borbiyaa	A type of marriage prevalent among the plains Tiwas.
Bordeo	Chief Priest, a distributor of offerings in a religious ceremony.
Bordhool	Big drum
Borhari	The eldest female of a *vamsa* in Tiwa society entrusted with socio-religious responsibilities.
Borjelaa	The eldest male of a *vamsa* in Tiwa Society entrusted with socio-Religious responsibilities, generally mother's eldest or youngest brother.
Borkhel Bichaar	A traditional system of dispensing justice in Tiwa villages.
Bormaal	Big bamboo or wooden posts.
Borgorokhia	Head of cowboys or boys who attend to cows.

Borotonis	The women who undertake fast in *Barat puja.*
Borsewa	A kind of puja held in the months of May/June.
Botaa	Traditional plate with stand generally used for offerings to god and to the guests.
Botaali	A chisel
Botol Maaji	A deity
Burabhakat	Office bearer of *Sasang ghar* (a sacred place where *rati sewa* ceremony is performed.
Buranji	Chronicles, History
Chaaloni	Bamboo made circular tray with holes, used to get rid of unwanted things.
Chaamaadi	Youth dormitory of Tiwa boys defunct in plains villages, but still active in hill villages.
Chaangdoloi	Leader of youth dormitory
Chaangi	Bamboo made temporary structure used to carry dead bodies.
Chaangmaaji	Next to *chaangdoloi* in command.
Chaapori	Land formed by riverine deposition.
Chaudang	An Ahom clan, the members of which were appointed to inflict punishments on criminals including sentences of death.
Chauraghar	An outhouse constructed a few yards away from the main house in a plains Tiwa village.
Chepaa	A kind of fish trap.
Chingrimai	A variety of paddy produced by wet cultivation.
Chok	A frontier outpost or entrance to a town duly fortified and garrisoned.
Choloukuthimai	A variety of paddy produced by wet cultivation.
Charaai	Bird
Chudrar	Container to serve rice beer.
Chulan	Container to serve rice beer on occasions.

Dakhraa paalas	Dancing with two long pieces of bamboo.
Damlong	A sub clan of the Tiwas.
Dao	A sharp cutting object.
Dekaajowaa	Term used in hill Tiwa villages when youth dormitory boys go for harvesting operations with accompaniment of songs and music to relieve monotony.
Dekaa Khel	Tiwa boys above fourteen years constitute this group.
Dekaarajaa	Surname of plains Tiwas men.
Deoraja	Surname of plains Tiwa men.
Deori	Priest
Dhaal	A shield
Dhanar Muthi Lowa	A ceremony performed at the time of sowing by the plains Tiwas.
Dharma	Religion
Dheep	Raised earthen platform.
Dhekeriani	Pertaining to lower Assam.
Dheki	Wooden log with pestle at one end used for grinding purposes, to separate grain from chaff.
Dhora	To catch
Dharaburhi	Traditional Rice beer which is made by adding water to the *juguli* after the first strong liquor is taken out. Also called *poniyaa mod.*
Digambaria	One section of *Raatisewaa* puja followers who do not wear clothes but wrap banana leaves in their bodies during the *sewaa.*
Dilamaari	An axle, a plough shaft.
Dingori	Fishing implement.
Dogora	A kettle drum.
Dol neta	Leader of a group.

Doloi	A priest
Dubari	A variety of grass used for religious purposes.
Dola	A sedan
Edhaar mod	Sufficient quantity of rice beer for members of a group.
Faamaari	Evil spirit
Gaamkhaaru	A bracelet
Gacha	An iron stand on which is placed earthen lamp.
Gaonburah	Village headman
Gaonkhowa	An official of the Raja (Tiwa chieftain).
Gayon-Bayon	A group of singers and instrumental accompanists.
Ghaabura	Eldest male of a *vamsa* in Tiwa society entrusted with socio-religious responsibilities, also called *borjelaa* and *jelaagabi*
Ghat	River bank
Giyaati	A mediator who is selected to carry out socio-religious rites on occasions of birth, marriage and death.
Gobhia	Resident son-in-law
Gogona	A small wind instrument made of bamboo
Gossain Ulowa Melaa	An occasion when the deity of a sacred place is taken on a procession
Gurunda	A kind of bird
Haadaari khel	A group of girls, women or men engaged in agricultural operations on a voluntary and reciprocal basis.
Haani Mora	Killing by piercing.
Haari Kunwari	Youngest female in a *vamsa* of a Tiwa society engaged in assisting *gharburaa* in *barghar.*
Haat	Market
Haathaam	Specific place of a clan in the cremation ground for cremation of its members.

Halon pothor	Spring
Hauri	Equivalent to *haadaari khel.*
Harna pothor	Summer season
Hukai	A clan
Huruma/Hurmphali	A designation given to a hill Tiwa youth of a youth dormitory entrusted with specific duties.
Jaakai	A fishing implement.
Japaa	An indigenously made suitcase used to keep things.
Jaap Soru	A type of utensil used by the plains Tiwas.
Jagat Juri	A deity
Jelaa	A priest
Jeth	The second month of the Hindu calendar corresponding to May 16 to June 15.
Jhum	Shifting cultivation
Jhura	A packet
Jol thol devota	Land and water deity
Joon Beel Mela	Animal fair held near Jagirod where barter system is in operation.
Jongkhong	A puja performed by the Tiwas before ploughing is undertaken for the year.
Jotora	A spinning object
Juguli	Boiled rice mixed with indigenous yeast called *baakhor* for preparation of rice beer.
Juskaai	A woven cloth worn by hill Tiwa women to cover the whole body from the breast to the legs.
Juwali	Harrow
Kaabla	Deity
Kaabya	Term used for husband of youngest daughter in hill Tiwa village

Kaachong	A woven piece of cloth stitched on two sides and worn by women to cover the lower portion of the body.
Kaahi naach	Dance with traditional plates made of bell metal.
Kailaash	Abode of Lord Siva.
Kaalikhaa	Deity
Kanchi	Sickle
Kanua	A variety of fish.
Karam	Ceremony performed after death in which food and rice beer are offered to the deceased by family members and others.
Kartik	Deity
Kathor Kaachowa	Preparing the land for transplantation of paddy.
Kekura dula	Curved Sedan
Kesaikhaati	A deity
Khaaji	Item prepared with fat of pig.
Khaandaar	Person who makes carvings of female busts, animals and birds on the cross beam of the *Chaamaadi.*
Khaaloi	Fishing implement.
Khaar	Alkali
Khaalaab	A bitter curry prepared with fat of pig.
Khaadi	Hand woven cloth of hand spun yarn.
Khaamela	The three individuals who wear sticks of flowers in *Sogra* festival.
Khaplang rawane	Pujaa performed before cutting of grass.
Kharlaaraw	*Haadaari khel* group of girls in hill Tiwa villages.
Kho	Bamboo made basket.
Khochapa	A bamboo made container to keep clothes.
Khoka	Bamboo made fishing trap.

Khomphor	Front verandah, place where loon is kept and also used for sitting purpose.
Khorala	Young girls of marriageable age.
Khordeng osa	Naming ceremony.
Khoricha	Bamboo shoot
Khorkia Panthai/ Khra Kura Panthai	Youth dormitory boys.
Khraam	Small drum
Khraambar	Big drum
Khumkaathis	The sticks of flowers which are put in the head gear of the three individuals in *Sogra* festivals.
Khuriphaali/ Khuriwaal	Designation of dormitory youths entrusted with specific responsibilities.
Kil Haadaari khel	System on a small scale.
Kuber	God of wealth.
Kachaa/Kechaa	Not black topped, a mud road
Kunchi	Bundle
Kul or Khul	Clan
Lagua	Person who caters to the needs of the Tiwa Raja.
Lakam	A poisonous herb
Laangkhun	A bamboo stick which is scraped finely from one joint to the other, used for dancing purposes.
Laangra	A unique gate of hill Tiwa houses.
Laathis	Sticks
Lengti	The strip of cloth worn at the waist by menfolk in hill Tiwa village to cover their private parts which is their traditional dress.
Lo/lo faap/lothaar	Ornaments
Loro	Priest

Maah	Gram
Maaju bhani	The middle sister
Maalbaaris	Bamboo post
Maangkhor	Cremation ground
Mahadeo/ Mahamai	Deity
Mai	Rice
Maidoswari	Newly harvested paddy kept in a pot.
Maajghar	A verandah in a traditional plain Tiwa house used for sitting purposes.
Maatir saal	A system of weaving where thread is kept tied to the waist, popular in hill villages.
Maiphui	Heap of paddy well covered in a paddy field.
Maiphur	Paddy stored in basket like structures kept in hill Tiwa homes.
Mai Rawa	Harvesting of paddy.
Mai Pothaalaa	Community threshing.
Mancha	Saturn
Meji	Heap of firewood burnt as a bonfire on the occasion of Magh Bihu.
Mela	Fair
Mewa libing hawe	Haadari khel group of men in hill Tiwa villages.
Midai	God
Mindu	Container where rice is boiled in hill Tiwa homes.
Missawa	Festival
Modaar	A variety of flower
Mahal	Person entrusted to make the *meji* in hill Tiwa village.
Mogondor Khoriya	Copper bangle
Morol pujaa	A kind of pujaa performed when a family member suffers form chronic illness.

Mothaal	Squirrel dance
Mouza	A revenue collection circle.
Mouzadar	Person in charge of a mouza.
Muhuri	A pipe
Muinaari Kaanthi	Festival of *Maagro* or *Maakro phoid* of hill Tiwas.
Nabanna	Ceremony in which solid food is given to the child for the first time.
Na bhuni	Nine sisters affiliations.
Naagera	A small kettle drum.
Naamghar	Prayer hall
Naam Kirton	Praise and prayer offered to Vishnu.
Naflangkhari	Vegetables cooked with *Sukuti.*
Nangal	A plough
Nara Chiga Khuwa	A feast on the last day of harvesting.
Nimai Chola	Shirt
Nirmaali	Flowers offered to God and then distributed among the devotees.
Noi	River
Noka kit	Rain song
Nomaji	The outermost room where male members take food in a hill Tiwa house.
Nowaan Jhawa	Community feast partaken by the Raja and his officers on the bank of Joon Beel.
Nubaar	Sacred place of hill Tiwas.
Nucha	Place used for sleeping purposes in *chaamaadi.*
Nukthi	Sitting area of *chaamaadi,* the room with the hearth in it in hill Tiwa house.
Nukur	Place used for storing firewood and implements.
Nunsiyoy	Backward and forward movement of dead body in foothill areas.

Paachrajia	The five Rajas of Topakuchi, Baropujia, Mikirgaon, Sorah and Khaigor.
Paachoni	Office bearer of *sasangghar.*
Paali	Assistant
Paangsi	Flute
Paariya	Rice beer, which is less strong equivalent to *dhoraburhi.*
Paarikha	Village messenger.
Pachoni	Office bearer of *sasang ghar.*
Paatchoura	Place where the Tiwa Raja changes clothes.
Panasawa	Blocking a river or stream to catch fish in hill Tiwa villages.
Paathisara	A variety of rice.
Patra mantris	Officials of Tiwa chieftains who undertakes duty in absence of the ministers.
Pauri	A kind of bamboo fish trap, *Haadaari khel* group of women in hill Tiwa villages.
Peraa	Big suitcase
Petaari	Small suitcase
Phaga	Turban or head gear of Tiwas.
Phangcho	A clan
Pharke	Blouse
Phagun	The eleventh month of the Hindu calendar corresponding to February 16 to March 15.
Phaskai	Woven cloth worn by females in hill Tiwa villages from the breasts to the knee.
Phoid	Clan
Phool Khati	A stick with flowers in it worn at the head gear during *Sagra missawa* of hill Tiwas.
Pinda	Offering of food and drink to the dead.
Pira	Raised wooden object used for sitting purpose.

Pirajuj	Fight with *pira*
Pichukhram	Small drum
Pitha	Rice cake
Paduli	Front portion to the entrance of a house.
Poghaa	Rope tied around neck of cow.
Pochotia	A variety of leaf.
Prabhat Pheri	Songs sung in procession along the roads of a town or village in the morning.
Prasad	Edible items distributed among devotees after offering to God.
Pukhuri	Pond
Punji	Village
Sa	Son
Saajaa	Daughter
Saajoni	Office bearer of *Sasong ghar.*
Saatrajia	The seven Tiwa Rajas of Baghara, Tetelia, Ghagua, Kumoi, Kacharigaon, Sukhnaguha and Tarani.
Sadya	Youngest daughter in a hill Tiwa family who inherits the lions share of property.
Saakori	Office bearer of *sasang ghar.*
Saalmari	A sharp edged agricultural implement.
Sandoh	Fried rice ground finely
Sangkranti	The last day of a month
Sange giri	Deity
Sanikeranne	A pujaa
Santaari	An official whose duty was to inform the Deoraja about any happening in his principality.
Santi Sena	An organisation formed during Freedom Struggle.
Saran	Initiation

Saraniya	Converted Neo-Vaishnavite
Satraadhikaar	Head of a *satra*
Satula Murti	A deity
Senpatia anguthi	A kind of ring
Sepat Thowa	To put in a hole, pertains to burial.
Sereki	Weaving instrument
Shagoni	Strainer for filtering traditional beer.
Sheristadar	A revenue official
Sigam pothor	Winter
Si	wife addressed by husband.
Siha	Ear-ring
Sil	Stone
Sil khongor	A deity of hill Tiwas.
Siliporoy	A deity
Sing la	Ornament worn by hill Tiwas
Sokpeera	A wooden object
Sokrakhori	Dried fish prepared with alkali.
Sogra	A clan
Sonane Khoriya	Gold bangles
Soron Kher	A variety of long grass required for roof of a traditional plains Tiwa house.
Soru Koch	Fresh converts to Neo-Vaishnavism.
Soru maal	Small sticks
Siu	Term used by wife to call husband, traditional rice beer is called by this term by the plains Tiwas.
Sukuti	Fish dried in a particular way and kept stored in long slender bamboos.
Taagla	Traditional waistcoat wom by tiwa menfulk.
Taamuli Doloi	An official whose duty was to supply areca nuts.

Taamulor dhakua	Outer cover of a betel nut tree.
Taanaa	The piece of cloth worn by hill Tiwa men at the waist to cover the private parts in the lower portion of body, also called *lengti.*
Tekela	Official who collected revenues from the public.
Telia Chareng	A bird
Thaan	A sacred large hall like structure used for religious purposes, generally in an out of the way place, near a forest.
Thokli	Pitcher to carry water.
Thongali	Waist band
Thunakhuta	The main post of *barghar.*
Thurang	Musical instrument.
Tiluaakheda	An official of *Buraa khel* in a plains Tiwa village in charge of musical instruments and dances of youths.
Tingri	Fishing trap
Tokaa	A musical instrument.
Tomaasi	Maagh Bihu
Tomere Kowa	Circle dance
Tukuri	A bamboo made basket.
Tumbang	A musical instrument.
Uraal	A husking pot with water in it, used to produce mock rain in times of drought.
Uwaal Burhi	Deity
Wanswaa	Festival of hill Tiwas.
Yaangli	Lakshmi Puja of the hill Tiwas.
Zu	Traditional rice beer

Bibliography

Primary Sources, Assamese

1. Choudhury, P.C. (ed), *Assam Buranji Sar* by Kashinath Tamuli Phukan and Radhanath Barbarua, DHAS, Guwahati, 1964.
2. Sarma, N.C. (ed) *Darrang Rajvamsavali*, Guwahati, 1973.
3. *Sri Sri Adijamal*, anonymous.
4. *Sukhnaguha Rajvamsavali* published by Jagat Singh Raja of Suknaguha Rajagaon, 1954.
5. *Moni Kunworor Akhyan* by Lakhi Singh Deka (unpublished).
6. *Nayan Kunworor Vamsavali*.

Secondary Sources (Assamese)

1. Barbarua, H., *Ahomar Din*, Guwahati, 1981.
2. Deori, M., *Tiwa Sa*maj, Assam Sahitya Sabha, Jorhat, 1983.
3. Deori, M., *Morigaon Jilar Lokasmriti*, Assam Sahitya Sabha, Morigaon, 1994.
4. Deori, S., *Smarak Grantha*, Morigaon, 2004.
5. Gogoi, L., *Tiwa Sanskritir Ruprekha*, Part I, Raha, 1986.
6. Gogoi, L., *Tiwa Sanskritir Ruprekha*, Part II, Raha, 1989.
7. Kalita, N, et. al, *Rahar Rahadoi*, Raha, 1980.
8. Kalita, B., *Phulagurir Dhawa*, Nowgong, 1961.
9. Kakati, P., *Gobhar Lalung Buranji*, Part I, Jagiroad, 1984.
10. Konwar, R., *Tiwa Sabda Sambhaar*, Assam Sahitya Sabha, Jorhat, 1981.
11. Kumar, S., *Eetihaase Suware Chashate Bachar*, Jorhat, 1980.

12. Panging, L., *Gobha Rajya*, Guwahati, 2004.
13. Pator, M., *Tiwa Sanskritir Jilikoni*, Tiwa Mathonlai Tokhra, Morigaon, 2004.
14. Sarma, U., et. al, *Jagi Bhakatgaon Anchalor Lokasmriti*, Morigaon, 2007.
15. Senapati, G.C., *Rahar Rahial Barua Aaru Paach Roja Powali,* Morigaon, 1997.

Magazines

1. *Enajoree*, Nellie, 2003.
2. *Gobane Thalar*, Tiwa Mathonlai Tokhra, 1995.
3. *Morigaon Sahitya Sabha Patrika,* Morigaon, 1980.
4. *Phera*, Tiwa Mathonlai, Tokhra, Jagiroad, 2000
5. *Ringchaang* Tiwa Mathonlai, Tokhra, Jagiroad
6. *Sangkhorla*, Tiwa Mathonlai, Tokhra, Jagiroad,2006
7. *Thuraang,* Tiwa Mathonlai Tokhra, Jagiroad, 2006.
8. *Thuri*, Tiwa Mathonlai Tokhra, Ulukunchi, 2002.

Primary Sources, English

1. Barua, G.C,. *Ahom Buranji*, Kolkata, 1930.
2. Bhuyan, S.K. (trans & ed), *Tungkhungia Buranji*, Reprint, DHAS, Guwahati, 1990.
3. Butler, J, *A Sketch of Assam with Some Account of the Hill Tribes*, London, 1847.
4. Census Reports.
5. Hamilton, F., *An Account of Assam*, DHAS, Guwahati, 1963.
6. Hunter, W.W., *A Statistical Account of Assam*, 2 Vols., London, 1879.
7. Jenkins, Francis, *Report on the Revenue Administration in Assam*, 1849-50, Kolkata, 1853.
8. Johnstone, J., *Captain Welsh's Expedition to Assam, 1792-94,* First edition, 1877, Shillong, 1912.
9. M' Cosh, J., *Topography of Assam*, Kolkata, 1837.

10. Mills, A.J.M., *Report on the Province of Assam*, 1854, Report, Publication Board, Assam, 1984.

11. Pemberton, R.B., *Report on the Eastern Frontier of British India*, First edition, 1835, DHAS, Guwahati, 1966.

12. Robinson, W., *A Descriptive Account of Assam*, Kolkata, 1841.

13. Sharma, B. (ed), *An Account of Assam* by *Dr. John Peter Wade*, North Lakhimpur, 1927.

Secondary Sources (English)

1. Acharyya, N.N., *North-east India in Historical Perspective*, New Delhi, 2006.

2. Aggarwal, K.S., *Dynamics of Identity and Intergroup Relations in North-East India*, Shimla, 1999.

3. Agnihotri, S., *The Lalungs*, Lucknow, 1996.

4. Bareh, H., *The History and Culture of the Khasi People*, Guwahati, Delhi, 1997.

5. Barman Santo, *The Raijmel – A Study of the Mel System in Assam*, Delhi, 2005.

6. Barooah, D.P., *Assam District Gazetteers*, Nowgong, Guwahati, 1978.

7. Barpujari, H.K. et.al (ed), *Political History of Assam*, Vol. I, Guwahati, 1977.

8. Barthakur, D.R., *The Music and Musical Instruments of North - Eastern India*, Delhi, 2003.

9. Barua, B. K., *A Cultural History of Assam*, Vol. I, Nowgaon, 1951.

10. Barua I., et. al, *Ethnic Groups, Cultural Continuities and Social change in North East India*, Delhi, 2002.

11. Barua. K.L., *Early History of Kamarupa*, Guwahati, 1966.

12. Baruah, S.L, *A Comprehensive History of Assam*, New Delhi, 1985.

13. Baruah, T.K., *The Singphos and their Religion*, Shillong, 1977.

14. Baruah A.K., *The Lalungs* (Tiwas), Guwahati, 1989.

15. Baruah, L.K., *Oral Tradition and Folk Heritage of North East India*, Delhi, 1999.
16. Bhuyan, A.C. et.al, (ed) *Political History of Assam, Vol.III,* Guwahati, 1980.
17. Beverley, H., *Census of Bengal*, 1872, Bengal Census Report, Kolkata, 1872.
18. Bordoloi, B.N., et. al, *Tribes of Assam*, Part I, Guwahati, 1987.
19. Bordoloi, B.N., *Transfer and Alienation of Tribal Land in Assam*, Guwahati, 1991.
20. Chatterjee, S.K., *Kirata Jana Kriti*, Kolkata, second edition, 1974.
21. Choudhury, R.D., *Archaeology of the Brahmaputra Valley of Assam*, New Delhi, 1985.
22. Choudhury, N.D., *Historical Archaeology of Central Assam from the earliest period to A.D. twelth Century,* New Delhi, 1985.
23. Choudhury, P.C., *The History of Civilization of the People of Assam upto the twelfth Century AD,* Guwahati, 1966.
24. Dalton, E.L., *Descriptive Ethnology of Bengal*, Kolkata, 1872.
25. Das, B.M., *Outlines of Physical Anthropology*, Delhi, 1990.
26. Datta, B., *Affinities between Folkloristics and Historiography*, Chennai, 2002.
27. Datta, P.,S., *Autonomy Movements in Assam,* (Documents), Delhi, 1993, ed.1.
28. Devi, L., *Ahom Tribal Relations*, Guwahati, 1968.
29. Downs, F.S., *Christianity in North-East India,* Delhi, 1983.
30. Dubey, S.M., *North-East India, A Sociological Study*, New Delhi, 1978.
31. Endle, S., *The Kacharis*, New Delhi, 1977.
32. Gait, E., *A History of Assam*, Kolkata, 1905, Guwahati, reprint of second edition 2005.
33. Gohain, B.K., *The Hill Lalungs*, Guwahati., 1992, *Continuity and Change in the Hills of Assam*, Delhi, 1994.

34. Gopalakrishnan, R., *Assam, Land and Her People*, Delhi, 2000. *Ideology, Autonomy and Integration in North-east India*, Guwahati/Delhi, 1990.

35. Goswami, A., (ed), *Traditional Self Governing institution Among the Hill Tribes of North-East India,* Guwahati, 2002.

36. Grierson, G.A., *Linguistic Survey of India*, Vol. III, Part II, New Delhi, 1967.

37. Jeyaseelan, Lazar, (ed), *Conflict Mapping and Peace Processes in North East India*, Guwahati, 2007.

38. Karotemprel, S., *A Brief History of Catholic Church among the Tiwas (Lalungs)* Vendrame Institute (Sacred Heart Theological College), Shillong, 1981.

39. Kumar, B.B., *The Tribal Societies of India*, Delhi, 1998.

40. Lamare, S.N., *Studies in Society and Change*, Delhi, 2005.

41. Mishra, U., *The Periphery Strikes Back*, Shimla, 2000.

42. Nath, R.M., *Background of Assamese Culture*, Guwahati, 1948.

43. Neog, M., *Anandaram Dhekial Phukan: Plea for Assam and Assamese*, Jorhat, 1977, *Sankardeva and His Times,* Guwahati, 1965.

44. Nyori, Tai, *History and Culture of the Adis*, Delhi, 1993.

45. Pakem, B., (ed), *Nationality, Ethnicity and Cultural Identity*, Delhi, 1990.

46. Pandey, B.B., *Leadership Pattern in a Tribal Society*, Delhi, 1991.

47. Playfair, A., *The Garos,* Guwahati, Delhi, 1975.

48. Riseley, H.H., *Tribes and Caste of Bengal, Kolkata,* 1822.

49. Saikia, N., *Assam and the Assamese Mind*, Jorhat, 1980.

50. Sarma, S.N., *The Neo Vaishnavite Movement and the Sattra Institute of Assam,* Guwahati, 1966.

51. Sen, Soumen (ed), *Folklore in North-East India,* New Delhi/ Guwahati, 1985, *Khasi Jainita Folklore*, Chennai, 2002.

52. Sen, Sipra, *Tribes and Castes of Assam*, New Delhi, 1999.

53. Sharma Thakur, G.,C., *The Lalungs (Tiwas)*, Guwahati, 1985.
54. Shyam Choudhury, N.K., and Das M.M., *The Lalung Society*, Kolkata, 1973.
55. Singh, G., *Ethno- Nationalism and Emerging World (Dis) Order*, Delhi, 2005.
56. Singh, N.J., *Ethnic Relations Among the People of North Eastern India*, New Delhi.
57. Singh, K.S., *People of India,* Assam Volume, XV, Part II, Kolkata, 2003.
58. Snaitang, O.L., *Christianity and Social Change in North-east India,* Kolkata, 1993.
59. Waddell, L. A., *Tribes of the Brahmaputa Valley,* Reprint, Delhi, 1975.
60. Walter Fernandes, Sanjay Borbora, *Changing Women's Status in India: Focus on North-east,* Guwahati, 2002.
61. Walter Fernandes, Sanjay Borbora, *Modernisation and Women's Status in North-Eastern India*, Guwahati, 2002.

Index

L

M

N